"Heller Levinson's Hinge Theory has shaken the foundation of what literature is / can / will become. I've anticipated each of his books ever since I was turned onto his brilliant Hinge Theory. Heller Levinson is one of the few contemporary poets whose work will be spoken of long after we have shuffled off this mortal coil. I consider Heller Levinson to be, without a doubt, one of the best poets of his generation and a poet whose work will be looked upon as one of the major chapters in American literature."

— Heath Brougher, author, editor, reviewer

"When drawing is allowed to create itself, to chart its own history and probe its own memory — and by doing so, to portend its future — the role of the artist is to step aside and witness. In a process of high fidelity listening, originality is revealed and Hinge occurs. Heller Levinson's *SEEP* brings us flush into an even more expansive display of the Hinge process where language segues to and from its own fertile environment. At witness in our ongoing collaboration between drawing and poetics is the experience of Hinge in two mediums. Line, the tangibility of space and voluble mark-making reflect themselves in the richness of their own possibilities and reverberate, rather than illustrate, the dynamic language of Heller Levinson's applications. *SEEP* vibrantly reveals the Indra's net of Hinge, casting a wide berth that extends to the cross-pollination of word, gesture, and the materialization of drawing."

— Linda Lynch

Seep

HELLER LEVINSON

Seep

Black Widow Press is an imprint of Commonwealth Books, Inc., Boston, MA. Distributed to the trade by NBN (National Book Network) throughout North America, Canada, and the U.K. All Black Widow Press books are printed on acid-free paper, and glued into bindings. Black Widow Press and its logo are registered trademarks of Commonwealth Books, Inc.

Joseph S. Phillips and Susan J. Wood, Ph.D., Publishers
www.blackwidowpress.com

Cover art: *Quarry, III* (detail) by Linda Lynch, Pastel pigment on cotton paper, 2015
Cover design: Linda Lynch
Art, page 2: *Quarry, III* by Linda Lynch, Pastel pigment on cotton paper, 2015
Art, page 14: *Empty Drawing* by Linda Lynch, Pastel pigment on cotton paper, 2013.
Book production: Kerrie L. Kemperman

ISBN-13: 978-1-7338924-4-5

Printed in the United States
10 9 8 7 6 5 4 3 2 1

"Contrary to what cultured people call good writing, it is by forcing the meaning of words, or else by shifting them, it is by twisting their usage, also by derailing coherent thought, it is by injecting gaps, disjointedness, margins and deviations, that we will produce the sole phenomenon worth seeking: the contribution of thought outside elements, the excess of the final product over the original stakes. It is by brutalizing words and principles, taking them by surprise, that we will obtain an explosion, a rebound, that we will make headway."

—Jean Dubuffet, from "Demagnetization of Brains."

"There can never be a straight line without curves intermingled."

—Leibniz

already there is noise.   among fictions a clause erupts.   wish

you were here.

Heller Levinson: Pro-Hinge, Protean

The danger crackles before the poet who wishes to *make it new,* tear down the walls, uproot the foundations, and let stream sunlight where once gloomed cinder-block, drab shades, asbestos, despite the myriad who called that structure a *Temple*, or *Helicon Central Banking.* Heller Levinson gambled, razed that imploding temple, and he found the gold ingots, incense and buried verb. Now, nearly two decades since he published *ToxiCity,* quickly followed by *Smelling Mary,* and then the explosion of books like *tenebraed* or *Lingua Quake,* Heller proves to be what most poets hope to achieve...he possesses his own voice, unique, unjaded...and he answers to himself only.

Heller Levinson: Protean...trailblazer...but by arduous tasks and initiation.

I first heard of Heller by way of Clayton Eshleman and Will Alexander. I was thrilled to hear of another poet in my Angelino environs. We met up often at a saloon in West LA. Notebooks filled with poems, ideas, we shared our work over cheeseburger plates, laughter, mugs of beer, and perfect synergy, and created new collages. By then—and I am speaking of 2003, or so—Heller had already crafted several open sequences prescient of his Hinge-method and fully formed voice. I still re-read his crow sequence, In *Stelliferous Eclipse,* and chart the poem's artful gauge on how to twist line-breaks, white-space, tensions between lofty and popular registers of language, melody and neologisms. (The poem was published in chapbook form by Unarmed Press.) Our sessions together resulted in a chapbook entitled *See-Saw.* I still return to it...

and I smile when, once in a while, I hear how so-and-so found it to be a collection touched by the marvelous.

Prior to those first open sequences loosening up Heller Levinson's breath and confidence in *doing it his way,* he was a traditional writer by the name of *James* Heller Levinson, and one who started off as a novelist to boot. The smooth-talking, handsome, worldly James Heller Levinson had settled in Los Angeles, leaving New York during the early 1980's. His keen intelligence and energy served him well in the still-profitable textile industry. (In the Great American Tradition of some poets—Stevens, Carlos Williams, William Bronk, Bert Meyers, Reznikoff—Heller knew of struggles other than the classroom and ivory, or ivy-covered, tower.) His years making bucks as a salesman resulted in a wild novel entitled *Another Line,* published and celebrated by the same press that brought out *Leaving Las Vegas.*

The book bristled with the razor-like narrative drive of Rechy or Miller. James Heller Levinson received some due recognition, yet he knew that that tradition—the Gonzo-New-Journalism-Pulp-Creative Non-Fiction—wasn't what he sought. (Shit! Even some Hollywood agent and screenwriter invited him to luncheon over starched tablecloths, ice-water, delicious repast and champagne at the Bistro, hoping that a movie could be made.) James had started writing poetry… well-honed poems in the American idiom, one pagers gathered in the chapbook *Pulled-Apart.* Poems had appeared in journals, which, back then, were what one could call the *usual suspects,* and where the celebrated, yet conventional voices, found themselves showcased. Yeats wrote how Joyce's first book of verse, *Chamber Music,* consisted of *words to be put to music perhaps,* and one could state that *Pulled Apart* contained poems to be spoken clearly recited and acted. They were convincing. Solid stuff. But again, James Heller Levinson had deeper rivers within.

I mention those two early volumes because, had Heller decided to pick the normal turnpike road in narrative work or poetry, he would have succeeded. His is a mind that absorbs everything. Nothing is wasted on Heller…and I know this from conversations. Philosophy, economics, history, anthropology…musical theory, hermeneutics, Paris, martial arts, animal behavior…the sheets of sound and associations rain endlessly. Heller could have remained James and now be teaching at some MFA factory, or PhD mill.

Perhaps the budge towards newness and the wildness can be gathered with the *Bad Boy Poems* published by the then-celebrated Bomb Shelter Press. The book—replete with lurid and goofy illustrations—possesses the fun and rawness of the best of Punk Music. If *Group Sex* by the Circle Jerks, or *The Ramones,* are quick and bracing yet electrifying LP's, then *Bad Boy* is in the same vein…but in verse. (I encourage readers to look up this book as well as Heller's sole novel to get the vast sweepings of his imagination and possible voices.) That poetry collection remains my son's first favorite poetry collection.

But to return to our *San Francisco Saloon* days: All of those experiments were done with accuracy and intuition. Like the great Modernists, like the plunges into *Ultraismo,* Cubism, *Creacionismo,* etc., Heller Levinson demanded new perspectives, unexplored diluvials hinging one trope to another and breaking open the azure hidden beneath black ink that spills the same oil-slicks in so many books and manuscripts seeping from MFA workshops. The folks at Howling Dog Press heard and published his *ToxiCity,* and then shortly thereafter, Heller came upon the Hinge Theory for composing poetry. Like Carlos William's "variable foot" or Wakoski's "deep imagism", the theory is both tangible and ether. But Heller has fellow writers working at the hinge method. And what matters more is that he had found his own trail, felled the dead trees and mud-mounds blocking his way. Soon thereafter, we find the insightful interviews with Heller Levinson as posted on *Jivin' Ladybug,* reviews in *Aught,* as well as celebrations of his work by visionaries like John Olson or George Kalamaras.

In addition to the books published by Black Widow Press, Heller Levinson has collaborated with Linda Lynch on artist book projects and cover illustrations. Her art radiates, an amalgam of Kline, Twombly, Agnes Martin, and the drawings of Gorky… the books, broadsides, and illustrations accompanied by text that Heller and Lynch have birthed are some of the most exciting creations in American Poetry and Art from the last twenty years.

In full form and flexing muscles, Heller's poems are untethered from any academic bullshit…they are the horror and beauty…weird, wonderful, sensuous…

tenebraed to
mermaid
to blue algae bludgeon slur
        scrape of solar scrim

or….

pounding
vacuum

lustre
baronial   burnish

baronial burnish discharge

fantasias inflame
the ash

or….

puffdaddy pencil point penitentiary perfidious prolix
puddle prank punk pucker

or…

The escape velocity of earth is 225,000 mph.

‘’’’

what entitles us to colonize other planets when we are
incapable of caretaking our own?

or…

pathos

… …

fade
collapsing

Unlike any *Gringo* poet from the States, Heller Levinson comes closest to those Latin Americans who molded magic and lava from moments of *jitanjáfora,* mixed with revelation…I am thinking of Mariano Brull, Pedro Mir famously in *Hay un país en el mundo,* and the celebrated nocturne of Villaurrutia. Never before, such melody….and sense…*sentido*…

I mention Mir while thinking about the collage of Heller strophes I composed quite randomly, just to illustrate how the riffs and bursts of sound also surge forth accompanied by satori. Heller Levinson is not a difficult poet…he is music, replete with envoi.

Heller Levinson: messages, frantic SOS from interstellar reaches, vacancies and ruptures of radiation, the real cosmic news, the intergalactic sandwich we all need to nourish our minds.

And now we have a new collection—*Seep*—and I am sure we will open a dynamite keg.

Most importantly, we have a clear trajectory of his visions and voyage. It hasn't been all *luxe, calme, et volupté,* but like that Spleen of equal brilliance, it all forms one book…stellar, solar, yet carboniferous, tellurian…or, just as the poet quips:

don't get
morbid, the
elevator
is
to
your
right

—**Anthony Seidman**

This appreciation first appeared in the Blog to the *Los Angeles Review of Books.*

Empty Meditations

vacuity

u(tt)(dd)erless

trussed, … tempered down

wearied bundle

terms of dismissal

how much of

emptiness

is

vacuous

how much of

vacuity

is

absence

vacuum pearlizes approach, braids

counter-institutional polestars,

gangrenes the slop

        of

                hoard

                ~

heard

                in the vacuum

→

                    →

lung

                ~

where in

emptiness

is

ballast

~

can we discriminate between vacuity & emptiness? . . .

~

tenebraed to

vacuity

to

pitted abeyance

stalled conveyor

accumulating wither

to the not that is not

(where in absence is reverb?

Oscillative flaps ashore like an endangered species, vocalisms

deprived of consensus tumble recklessly netted in obloquy,

hazard churls the scintillative

the disappearance of whistling

hardly matters

"the red barn is empty" would not signify that the red barn participates in the notion of nothingness, rather, that the red barn contains no matter, is void of contents. that it is spacious, wide open, . . . available.

for a red barn to symbolize emptiness it would have to unoccupy its place as a red barn.

does color establish presence?

emptiness emptied is vacuum

imagine an empty clarinet

~

how much of

'lost'

is

emptiness

empty = without

emptiness = the void ploughed clean,

a draft drizzling incinerate,

the evaporate

evisc-

er-

ating

how much of

emptiness

is

disposable

soused in the lip-churl chasm gasp of a blunted asperity

this

concupiscence newly,

a ruddy

totter assembly

a reconstitution

oxygenating

from bramble & bush

birch & bear

breezing through causeways

marsh

& arcanum

tooled to conspirator

to twilight dorados

spatial marauders

emptying

            the

empty

providential was a way of life not without its rewards
albeit justly jollity jujube on all fronts foci joint of view
preliminaries upheld swell pondered over among
disciplinarians kneecaps offer distinction a point of contract
disturbingly pestilential just to point out why pester with
subordinates when the perpendicularity of ruthless serves as
a cheat sheet the betting man pays out a moment of silence
for the bamboo rake ground-filing a filigree a pedigree
purloin purple not a color addicted to weight-loss the law of
averages supply side economics after effects after all
lampoon buttery instability tricolating early this year proper
skin care retards aging
boot   saddle
elk
it's been a long time

that bafflement

convalescing

among abysses

with

soft edges,

coating

the undersides

of a

well-stitched

heel

. indisposition ceremonializes constraint

. the far side is the near side overlooked

. wishing to un-wrinkle the neck

. approximation caretakes inevitability

. conjecture = the root of construct

. disappearance as an art form

. death: the disappearance par excellence

how much of

silence

is

sad

nostril ladder spittoon bathe lozenge silk

the leather

of

space

potentialities pucker for purchase

irregularity suds

mixed company

the fruit of

compliance

Tercaquarium

the snowy floor of the hog's pen

rattling at dawn

the slow flesh of underlip

~

the discharge was

medieval but not

without volume

~

across

the border

not much

~

unaccountably

the stumble

produced

~

rambunction

runs

… runs

~

pulsation collared

curbed

perturbed

~

trellis swell

rotted wood

the magic of cards

~

heard

in the vacuum

lung

~

it couldn't have been otherwise.

rendition is a form of trust.

& for trust to fail, . . . well.

~

mouths mouth.

crumbs crumble.

it's never much more than that.

~

what alone is non-cancellable

thirst

summation

~

among mist surrey feather the unclaw pads what

matters most urging shape

speech an ability to dissimilate

~

among moose stalks jitterbug through

crests of sienna vermilion rugby grass the

dented hills under arrest

~

among attenuation the climbing stalled

figures of configuration wax to certitude in the days when

cleanliness mattered

~

among frame the deterioration nowhere in sight

subsequently the wages backfired all along the roadway

chuckling

~

"Birds are flowers flying,

and flowers perched birds."

Birds are birds

& flowers are flowers

doesn't anyone say *glade* any more

Oh, . . . if only

A play

Character:

A well-built middle aged athletic-looking man in relatively good shape seated a little shy of stage front / center in a basic armless wood chair. He wears a white sleeveless t-shirt, khaki pants, & white old-timey tennis sneakers.

Stage black, lighting comes on slowly, focuses on nameless male figure. His head is resting on his fist, reminiscent of The Thinker, *shuffles his feet, lifts his head, moves it about, as if trying to figure something out, get a grip on things.*

Man: I don't know, I don't know, I think I'll go for a stroll *[stays seated, but shuffles his feet, shifts about]* . . . it's times like this . . . wish I weren't . . . I don't know . . . honest to god . . . for the sake of Pete . . . if only I could . . . then . . . there's the rub, that's it, isn't it? if only, . . . then . . . who wouldn't . . . faced with that . . . who wouldn't want to look at it that way . . . I mean, given the option, what're you gonna do . . goin around like that . . . who wouldn't . . . most likely . . . so to speak . . . it's the goin that gets you somewhere . . . takes you along . . . picks you right up . . . takes you there . . . I mean, who wouldn't . . . in a manner of speaking . . . to say it like that . . . ***that's it*** *[man immediately sits up, straightens his back, springs to life, spreads his arms & hands out]* putting it out there . . . there's the thing, the thing of it . . . I mean, there's no doin without doin, ain't that the truth, the bum's rush, the pickle's juice, ain't that right *[in a slow studied fashion (almost timid) actor arises from chair, shuffles about a bit, grows in confidence, straightens his back]* gettin on with it . . . I mean there's no doin if you can't be gettin on with it . . . I mean it beats gettin old . . . a bunch of old sour pusses, that's what they are . . . that's what the old are good for, gettin sour & *[says the next firmly]* **stayin sour** . . . that's why you've got to pull up your pants *[yanks up his pants]* & get on with it . . . the spittin image my god . . . & what's the good of that I ask you . . . like we said, it's the gettin on . . . one foot ahead of the other *[man does this]* . . . that's it *[grows excited]*! step by step . . . who, who would've thought . . . to pull it off like this . . . just like this . . . a work of . . . well god knows . . . that's the rub . . . you know, move it about a little *[gingerly begins to feel space with his limbs]* . . . rub a dub dub . . . there ya go . . . 3 ducks in a tub . . . jus' movin' . . . that's it . . . that's all . . . this that . . . that this . . . there you go . . . there you go . . . rub a dub dub . . . movin' about . . . that's all . . . wish I could . . . you know, . . . I mean it might be possible . . . if only . . . & then you chance it . . . you know, you've got to chance it . . . there's no beatin around, no playin about . . . no other way to put it . . . there ya go . . . I mean, sittin around bein' sour, what's the use in that . . . I ask you, what's the use in that . . . there ya go, here you have it . . . what's the use in that, I ask ya . . . you got to light out, jus' go, . . . go . . . there's no other way, in a manner of speakin I mean, . . . no other way to put it, . . . ya jus got to light out, that's all . . . jus sayin it ain't gonna do much good, jus' thinkin' ain't gonna help neider, *[his pace slackens, begins to slow, slowly descends to sit in his chair again]*. . . got to light out *[voice lowers, says it a few more times to himself, diminuendo, body starts sagging forward, reverting to position curtain opened up on, lights dim]* light out   light out . . . that's what I say, . . . jus' gots to light out

[stage black]

[lighting appears slowly, man has his feet stretched out, arms crossed, . . . now he comes off very collected, unlike the opening where he appeared vulnerable, in mental disarray . . . he is sure of himself now, almost cocky, stares at audience with an air of superiority, haughty . . .]

Man: think I know somethin', don'chya? I know . . .

(aggressively)

I know what I know dat's what I know . . . it gets me around . . . & then some . . . that's what I know . . . for all the good it'll do'ya . . . what else, but gettin around, . . . more of that where that came from . . . for all the good it'll do ya . . . works for me, I do alright . . . get around, what's not to like, a penny for your thoughts, *(jiggles around a bit, lighten's up)* a farthing for a tale, ... ha! . . . for all the good it'll do ya . . . the long & tall of it . . . there's the rub . . . why's everone got to be doin' somethin' all the time, do this do that, . . . go here, there . . . what's to it anyways . . . there's the rub . . . where you goin' . . . go here go there, what's the difference . . . goin. . . is there any difference, . . . there / here, this way / that . . . twiddle dee / twiddle dumb . . . there's the rub, . . . that ole folk tale, the lightin out . . . all there is to it . . . the lightin out . . . this way / that . . . hunky dory, there ya'go . . . the buck stops here, the all of it . . . looks you right in the face it does . . . donch'ya know . . . yup, as they says in the army, front & center, yup, *(more loudly)* front & center boys! that's it right there, right in front of ya, the all of it, it all adds up, . . . that's where it goes, front & center, the all of it, little lambs eat ivy, the whole whopper, now ain't that the truth . . . rub'a dub dub . . . the sum total . . . sure as I'm standin' here *(looks down at chair & realizes he's not standing)* an old wive's tale . . . yessir's the sum total, the whole enchilada, right there, in front of you, starin'ya right in the face, donchya'know . . . you can see it in your dreams, in your dreams, clear as spades ... & then some . . . put that in your pipe & chew on it . . . why not . . . a figment of you 'magination . . . there it is, been there all the time, starin'ya right in the face . . . peek a boo I see you . . . you know, sometimes, . . , *(pause)* I'm jus thinkin', sometimes I don't know what I'm sayin, I mean, what's the use you know, like what my sayin is sayin, maybe not much, maybe not much at'll, so what's the use, what's the use of sayin if sayin ain't sayin much , . . . I'm jus, after all, whaddya got? what else is there to it . . . the short & tall of it, so to speak . . . no other way, but there isn't is there, . . . this is what we got, this sayin . . . for better or worse . . . thar she goes . . . way down yonder in who knows who knows, . . . it goes like this, topsy turvy, baah baah black sheep, stick that in your pipe & sheep on it . . . play me for a fool do'ya, . . . well, we'll see we'll see . . . I'd best be goin' lightin' out . . . nowhere as fine a time as now . . . don't know where I'll be goin. . . but I'll be goin . . . better yet, when I'll get there . . . gotta set out . . . clear my head, the all of it, ya'know, so to speak, . . . how to reckon . . . the tall the short, the lean the fat of it, it's all the same . . . London bridge is falling down . . . I mean, when you look at it, what's the point . . . the whole friggin point of it all . . . in a manner of speaking . . . little lambs eat ivy . . . you can't have it both ways . . . the way I see it . . . lookin at it that way . . . jus stares you right in the face it does . . . no blinkin no sneakin 'roun . . . right there in front of you, jus lookin atch'ya . . . whaddya gonna do . . . fetch a ball? squirt a gun? . . . jus think about it, I mean c'mon . . . jump a clue . . . goose a gander . . . getta load . . . sprinkle me wisely spare me sparsely . . . which way ya'gonna go . . . I mean, what's the difference, so to speak . . . how to reckon . . . what's the point of it all . . . what's the point to it all . . . if you're ever in Seattle . . . drop the ball . . . I mean there's a curve if ever I saw one . . . all dressed up & all . . . ain't she lovely . . . whaddya gonna do . . . who cares . . . who cares anyways . . . nobodies really . . . *(gradually becoming less sure of himself)* . . . take it like that, to the left the right, all there is to it, right there in front of ya, always is, not like it's goin disappear or nuthin, . . . in a manner of speakin, a way of sayin dontchya know, . . . I mean you go through all this & whaddya got . . . I don't know . . . I need to be goin . . . *(more quietly)* I really jus don't know, . . . I need to be goin

[lights fade as man slowly asssumes his initial posture of The Thinker*]*

where in

abandon

is

approach

gone

gone but gone away go

but . . . . . who . . . . . . where

gone . . . . go . . . . . . but . . . . go where . . . . go

gone go what when go way

where but . . . . if .... but who . . .

when

. . . how then where go gone then

go go .... *(gully swap)* .... *(crocodile)* . . . go

if when how then now there

then when but if

then how go go go

gone where where go

but how if but .... when

where how then now now then

go this go this go go gone

this when when where this gogo

this this go go there go gone gone go

go go

shadow stravage

unsealed unsubstantiated

peeled from surface

gone askew chortling

unstrung

a shadow unfolding re-

composing as

non-affiliate

a lurk

in consummate

consideration

a-paginate

this better not least for worst hardly

better yet you might have tried

in a manner of speaking that says it all

come clearly come light come hardy hardly

come rightly come sprightly

in a manner of speaking

or

you might not

come at all

folly for to seem

folly for to seem to need to see seeing over there this here

what is afar afaint over there here this there word folly given

glimpse & where from away for to to what this folly word

afar afaint from glimpse from seem all this need to afaint

away afar over there this here from what given word given

here there away the word to glimpse seeing the word where

what word where afar afar glimpse see where given here the

need to seem afaint what folly see for the need to seem to

see all this this all seeming

word over there

afar afaint   see

far far to

to seeming

what

pith-fully

You wish to know what is going on inside things and yet you are content to view them from outside; you wish to savor the pith but stick at the bark. — Franz Von Baader

bore   bore fit-ful   crust-crash-

crumb   rake-drill-transpierce, spike

pour into

leaven

in   ter   i   or   i   ty

d

e

l

v

i m m e r s e

desuetude   drill bulge

mag-ni-fy

p a s s a g e

— plush pulsative

— tilt hover

— veer: vacancies

itinerant transparencies

latched respirations

proceed

unyielding

ventilative

passage: let us pause over the word 'passage, ' (used in the application above) particularly the first syllable 'pass' which is honored to have one of the longest definitions in the English dictionary. Among the considerations 'pass' offers as it relates to 'pith-ful-interiority,' is the notion of extension, of going beyond, despite hardship & obstacles. The epiphanic fallout as it relates to Hinge is prodigious: One could begin by viewing a pass as a permission slip for the 'term' to enter, access granted to move about freely, to defixate from the lexicon & ex(pan)(ten)d. Once mobilized, the 'pass' simulates the transference a relay racer engages in when he 'passes' the baton to another runner, an action analogous to what happens in HT when the 'term' experiences/undergoes multiple modular transfers as it advances from one module to the next, accruing density & depth (mileage) with every transfer. Embedded in the act of transfer is the chemistry of transition, a further component of pith-ful activity.

We might now begin to inquire how pass passes into passageway, & how would it be advantageous to view passageway, . . . a narrow corridor leading to explosive revelations as one emerges to the marvel of the painted galleries in a Paleolithic cave only after having endured crawling long stretches on one's belly? Or the 'passage' as a metaphysical routing, as a leading to, as the Way of the Pass?

smote gradation

veer buffet slap   incurable ring

ing   bootlegged ditties appeal for cauliflower

pangs of an over-anxious orthodoxy

drool collusion

inkspots

delirium tremens

erotic echo

prurient ombudsman

days like this

than the sprint

no place

like home

spate rendition

splash sumptuosity   rectify

the earnest alarmed

regulations in disrepair

supply systems jammed   gardening no

longer precious but prosperous

seeds hardy

                hardly an

oversight overlooked

the 5 string banjo –

amazing

smoke lavender

jodhpur joust   rubs

      pleat periwinkle

skin-scented joineries,   , flush

with intimacy, with

keyed murmuration . . . . . .

. . . .

parcels congregate

embellish rotation . . .

. . .

wind as

suffix

how much of

memory

is

residue

Dialogics: **The Dialogics are ongoing conversations between Will Alexander & Heller Levinson. They initiated in 2001 in Los Angeles over beer & burgers at 'The Saloon' on Pico Boulevard. Below is a recent sampling.**

H: When you ask what advice I would offer a poet seeking to develop, I would most emphatically steer them away from creative writing programs, MFA's, & other assorted capitalist ghettoizations. Instead I would suggest internship with a master. An example of what I have in mind would be the Iditarod. Imagine having the opportunity to apprentice with the champion musher Lance Mackey. Imagine the sheer variety of educational nuggets such an immersion could provide: you would have to become intimate with, — weather, topology, terrain, husbandry, canine intelligence / psychology, how to access & train that intelligence, as well as feeding, nutrition (for the dogs as well as oneself), physical & mental conditioning for hardships, for successes, for failures, a knowledge of gear, of pattern & determination, — the sheer potential for multi-directional growth is astounding. Plus, rather than having to apply for a scholarship or shelling out big bucks, you might actually earn money (Lance actually *paid* his helpers). It's so exciting I might intern myself.

W: The Iditarod being a blinding dissertation on consciousness. Every aspect leading to multiple other aspects. I just spoke of this exfoliating realia to my students for almost four hours last evening about the intensity of the zeitgeist and its attendant shadows and how to write one's consciousness into light. Not only navigation through the pitfalls of language, but igniting one's motion via instantaneous kinetics. The various generosities of Being need be exercised and explored so that one's language begins to exhibit a protracted malleability while at the same time condensed by the beauty of compounding. In short, an alchemical panoply that includes both and wavering providing essential medicine for one's character. Language must take the activity of clairaudience, of a spell disengaged from quotidian satisfaction. Not a mirage, where each word will have been immersed in sattvic wattage, so that they collectively ring according to a scale of illumination. A glow rather than an adolescent inferno where specifics emerge magnetized by the spell of uranium orientation. But first, the practitioner is tested by failure, by the shadow of seeming non-result, by general loss of the non-essential, worn, clinging to crags in order to secure survival. This being the earnestness of search, of protracted renewal, of boiling orientation, transmuting the quotidian according to what I've coined as a living scape of lyrical statistics.

H: So, the road to 'ignition' road, to identify those generosities, to cosy-up & roll with same, to Hinge-Gather-Compound-Burst from inflammatory surfeit with spillage alchemizing as the very sauce of plasmic welfare. When you speak of 'tested by failure,' I am, of course, reminded of Beckett who advises to "fail better." And with 'boiling orientation,' I envision those sled dogs with their thirsty slathering tongues, their cracked & frozen paws (even with their booties on), their blazing eager eyes lunging toward a finish line, not entertaining, as far as I know, any thoughts of an

NEA grant, or some quotidian prize, but latched to a pursuit that exceeds them, to a thrill that installs rooted vivacity as the dance of the earth.

Our notion of the 'finish line' has to be redefined as well as re-designed. We will do this as we go along, not by pointing, but through suggestion, molding, shaping, . . . planting.

how much

glow

permeates

shadow

how much of

shadow

participates in

glow

how much of

glow

glows through

seepage

how much of

spillage

is

slippage

let us meditate upon the kinetics of: spillage :/ /: slippage

:/ /: = a see-saw sign

how much of

spillage

is

prosperity

how much of

slippage

spills into

seepage

W: If we think in strict financial terms it can be too much leaving or too much coming in. In terms of loss or intake it is too often associated with money or manufacturing. Never is the higher plane invoked concerning spillage as release from one's containment as an ego. On the material plane spillage is seen as a loss. As something from which one needs recover. Spillage is always a material consideration. Prosperity seems never a concern other than matter. In this sense it remains confined perfection or an overreaching menace. It never concerns the plane that is anterior and / or ascends above it. This latter condition of the anterior remains sans nouns or linear scripting takes on the character of a hallucinated posture. A posture not unlike germination of infinite prosperity. I am not speaking in terms of quantity but of motion as Divine conundrum. At a lesser level seepage foretells this flow. It remains the alchemy as mote in confined human space, and transmutes to poetic grammar of profound immeasurability. It remains as pluvial kinetic that alchemically refines and generates greater human perspicacity.

H: I love that we're addressing what I title the Linguistically Undocumented, — terms that are underappreciated, underattired, that slip below the cultural radar. When these terms do come attired, they appear in the guise of Uniform usually associated (as you point out) 'with money or manufacturing.' This brings to mind the doctor in Virginia Woolf's *Mrs. Dalloway,* who says "health is *proportion* (italics mind)."

> Worshipping proportion, Sir William not only prospered himself but made England prosper, secluded her lunatics, forbade childbirth, penalized despair, made it impossible for the unfit to propagate their views until they, too, shared his sense of proportion . . . .

These proportionate constraints are what mortify the human spirit, castrate the soul. As I have mentioned in various Hinge discussions, when the Logos becomes fully maturated, blush with liveliness-es, the natural impulse is to release, — to splinter/spill/slip from the impregnated 'term' to *seep* these enriched nutrients into a greater 'pluvial kinetic.'

tenebraed to

seepage

to the vertebrae of disappearance

disparities columnize in lopsided disarray

densities convulse

calibrations formatting the well-heeled wither in inebriate

perambulation

from these halls of cirrhotic séance

loams the

first heard

a pedal's reminiscence

comatose glucose rye toast you the host cool coast bel-
licose roast boast crull corollary extraordinary teary eerie
fives on the theory jive a-live Bedford Stuy --- -ve----sant vice
verse terse reimburse slant slide spell it out shout about cull
caul call glare declare use clout pout no doubt redouble your
trouble reboot your cahoots rumble your humble don't step
on the stumble fantasize fiction friction fricassee fromage
fantail romance-sail glor-ify magni-fy you see I see
we see
ya see

Shadow in Transliteration

a crude comp upon patterns of

disfigure, . . . iterations

stalled, emptied of

salt. along the way

glaze dispatches, . . . the

porcelain

pitcher thirsty for

light, for

solubility built

upon brick

brood like ambidextrous void

roiled incongruities roll out

a

slash-conspiracy dismembers

a

hover strains,

the

unsightly wedge barely,

markings

fail their indication

— respite under the sun —

perplexity

a subject for predication

thresholds

volume

brood askew

leery of

assignment

leafy with

a

drained

wisdom,

inveterate

underlyer teems a spent calculus

a

stalled filtration

a

reiterant

sedimentation

brood in attenuate fever

surplus stripped to cleat-trench, to

circumferential collapse, → cyclonic

funnel torqueing to a condensed am-

algamate. the other side of persuasion, a

flotation pinwheeling through longitudinal

tear-downs, system wrecks, a-

rhythmic nomenclatures. itinerancy

corrupted, fever

stitches

to a

stammering octave

brood in attenuate fever diagnosed

The ambition of the above poem is to trace the neural mechanics of the mental state *brood* through the medium of language. Although the sole laboratory for conducting this operation is the author's mind, he believes that there is an overlapping commonality if not coincidence among others' mental states.

By beginning with the word 'surplus,' the first line represents how brood initiates with a tucking-in, a siphoning away from a more generalized consciousness, is *stripped* to a more focused & gathering intensity, a *cleat-trench.*

Brood cocoons one cyclonically into a bouillabaisse of considerations, *condensed amalgamate.* One hovers in suspension while entwined in discernments, floats in the toss of the indeterminate in which the usual signposts don't apply, resulting in: *longitudinal tear-down, system wrecks, etc.* This dynamic between the urgency to achieve conclusivity while brewing in the inconclusive is partly responsible for the intensity so identifiable as 'brooding.'

While being compelled to unravel this complexity, to arrive at some determination, one is shackled to the pursuit, unable to wander off, in a condition of *itinerancy corrupted.*

Now, the title: the fever is an *attenuate* fever. It is rarefied because it is not dispersed but is rather spun into spiral, the very motion of the brood. The outcome is the *fever* of brood abating by attaching itself to something, even though that identifiable 'something' stammers with vulnerability.

brood quicks from the folds of despair

lurches locutions & stirrings ripe

pounces upon the drape of shadows bright

intent to reel the shape of things for repair

an urge to unravel to travel far for care

this prodigious fare rarely sought

a populace that values only the bought

which caters solely to the sight.

annul the findings that leave no trace of tear

that spring ceaseless uncounseled & flip

for casually they will fail to appear

when summoned for ripe leadership

brood deep for the flourishes that wear

that banner husbandry & kinship.

upon reflection it's pointless to consider alternatives in the wake of administrative fallacies the derelict the disbeliever the denuded the disgraced the downtrodden it's moments like this when opportunities abound boundless bosom broth bramble bumble don't ya know *yet* perimeter science has arrived at a subversion of terms based upon scrupulously unfolding nightgowns & other diverse theories a complexion of parts bearing granular perplexities if only you stayed for the finale the uproar was uproarious it was the driest of seasons the dreariest poultry if tutorials could account for Sunday football the kinetics of beer slippery when wet watch where you step the game wardens came up empty the game never came the art of trespass is experiencing a revival in inner circles otherwise why waste the paint it's a species of discontent to pray for salt after hours a dark space between the evidence looms large rehearsals are fumbling the influence of outsiders cannot be overstated still the morning hours delicious for fornication

dark to bark across

elongative fealty   spatial

bruise   caliper crunch

c a l i b r a t i o n

distance: a series of sums

dark: intumescence

the lute arks splashes tropical

discharges . . . confides

a legato loses its way

Rumination Upon: 'dark to bark across'

Honoring 'elongative fealty,' we note the 'arc' in both 'dark' & 'bark,' a combined semantic / sonic pairing, a bridge of sorts. How would the poem shift if 'ark' were substituted for 'bark?' How do 'bark' & 'dark' inter-influence one another across the instrument of distance? What sort of bark? A canine bark? If so, how would it sound? Would it be the short-clipped high-pitched sound dogs issue when curious, cast into the perplexity soup to fetch resolution? To chew on a comfort bone? How does 'across' create distance? Does it darken the darkness? How do 'bark' & 'across' act as a combined elongation mechanism to stretch-out the composition of 'dark?' What would the poem be like if 'through' was used instead of 'across?'

How does 'bark' affect the complexion of dark? Does 'bark' bruise the 'dark?' puncture the 'dark?' blush the 'dark?' cause the 'dark' to tremor, to vibrate with mystery? Does 'bark' personalize 'dark?' Make it more intimate? Is bark a mobilizing agent enabling the poem to revolve? How would the poem feel if 'bark' was understood to be the 'bark' of a tree? a small sailing vessel?

What do the terms 'caliper crunch' & 'calibration' tell about the nature of distance? A bark has a limited acoustical range; does that restriction affect darkness's extension? Is there a subject of 'endurance' emerging? Is distance distance if it's immeasurable? Do instruments of measurement threaten to stagnate a revolving composition? Does the introduction of the lute add color to the sonic orchestration? Does the verb 'arks' strategically link the lute to dark & bark in a spirit of a caroling consortium? Does the lute appear theatrically, like a dancer leaping in from off-stage, emoting into the darkness before fading away? Is the legato lost as in directionless, or is it consumed, enveloped in intumescence? Or could it be 'gone' as in the 60's term, 'far out?'

Since the above rumination is based on a series of questions, could we visualize the 'query' as a bark across the dark?

bark across the dark

ferocity flung

        fling current

                slide trombone

improbable fetch

a fugue

thins, ignorant

of collapse

how much of

meditation

is

query

....

where in the

query

is the

meditation

The Blue Armchair

A Play

CAST: The Blue Armchair

The following text appears on a screen in front of a closed curtain:

the blue armchair expresses blue as well as
comfort.

the heretics fled. the bushes filled with spies. the
weather puckered.

the blue armchair oozes leisure. solace. the blue of the
armchair swells. asserts itself as blue. swells with invitation.

the blue armchair stuttering in
complexity wraps itself in mood.
blue mood.

the blue armchair concerned about acquiring complacency fictionalizes crimson.

the blue armchair was nothing if not a blue armchair.

often uncompanionable. often uncomfortable with being occupied. much of the time the blue armchair was defined by dissatisfaction.

when the blue armchair was feeling unsociable, it was neither a hindrance nor a deprivation. it did, however, require accommodation.

such an 'accommodation' – for the blue armchair, plunged into consternation, sunk into a deep funk — was often provided. by, in the evening, a weighty posterior sinking into the fabric & distributing the disturbed muddle.

just suppose, thought the armchair, if I could honor my aversions, if, say, repulsed by a certain person, I could summon the power to reject them, to be able, as soon as a revolting posterior posted upon my comfort station, to eject them into the atmosphere, send them hiking.

Such ruminations served to comfort the armchair.

alternatively, Blue mused over an agreeable perhaps deliciously succulent posterior, . . . alluring, temptious, provocative. Such a presentation would reverse the impulse to repel with the desire to compel: compel to prolong, to bask in, to become a part of, join, … fuse, to sensuously soak, swallow, to glow in the glissades of amour. Would incite the urge to persist rather than dismiss.

These bipolar considerations did not stress Blue.

S/he embraced supple.

Curtain Opens:

Front center a blue armchair. Off stage, a voice speaks for the Blue Armchair:

crumbs. crumbs cause me distemper. they are the refuse of refusal. the refusal to consider. the other. what an other might find objectionable. insupportable. insufferable. probably a major cause for my discomfort at being in this household. with inconsiderate persons. insufferable. well, the wife is not so bad. she's not prone to crumb me. but then, she rarely sits upon me. at least, not with anything resembling regularity. He, on the other hand, & maybe it's a gender thing, is predictable & insufferable. did I use that term before? insufferable? perhaps a queer word for an armchair to articulate given that an armchair, myself in this case, is manufactured for sitting. Yet, there is sitting & then there is sitting. or should I say, plopping. plopping is formless. lack's class. gracefulness. yes, the he of the household is a plopper. bona fide.

Sundays are the pits. especially during football season. He gets all tense. If he's in the kitchen I can sense it. his agitation. his eagerness. as if a lot depended upon the outcome. as if it would personally impact his life. perhaps it does. I don't know. but I do know it impacts mine & I suffer. there goes that word again — *suffer, insufferable* — no way to beat it, I suffer the vicissitudes of the game. if it's going his way, kicks to my lower parts along with loud shouts of hurrah. things go bad, I get rock hard fists slamming into my arms. not to mention when his hands & arms are flailing the crumbs are flying. flaking down into my interiors. highly *un*comfortable. insufferable. then there's the beer & the suds. spilling. soaking. upsetting my upholstery. wet. soggy. miserable.

mornings like this I want to be elsewhere. what am I but a crumb-doused blue armchair reeking of beer & deposits of overbearing flatulence. a fetid chunk of disregard. yeah, the slob fell asleep after the football game & didn't rouse until after midnight. luckily it's a workday & I'll have time to recover. perhaps the pain wouldn't be so severe if I didn't have a comparison. my former home before this was with a quiet, elderly couple who were meticulous in their habits. I was always clean, my cushions fluffed. hardly ever sat in. & I was often spoken of. in the most flattering terms. I felt cared for, . . . desirable. but they moved to a retirement home, moved me to the Salvation Army where fatso moved me here. dreaming of elsewhere is difficult. especially when I have no idea where that elsewhere would be.

Ok. Okay okay okay . . . there's got to be a way out of here. but there isn't. I am not like people, I can't get on buses, cars, airplanes . . . take off, vanish. I can't even play video games, I have no cell phone, no like-minded souls to console with. all I have is this dreadful monologue. this endless speech. speech can let you down. can be the end of you.

when speech fails, . . . what? that final cry tumbling toward nothingness. sucked into vacuum. when that final cry, that last heave, can no longer be brought forward, that last utterance forsaken, voided, . . . what then?

this morning I awoke feeling contradictory, — not in a white sock/brown sock kind of way, mind you, but more in a having to do with self-worth kind of way . . . a feeling of dissatisfaction with myself, sort of like, how shall I put this, . . . okay, I'll just put it, — I felt *uncomfortable.* this may seem like a small thing, a not very big deal to some, for, clearly, persons are feeling uncomfortable all the time, — including myself, as I have mentioned — for various reasons, such as: physical discomforts — hunger, cold, hot, crumbed — inadequate clothing, poor mattresses, embarrassments, etc., so why was my discomfort — a feeling which was by no means novel to me — at this point, at this point of awakening, so striking, so 'contradictory' as I braved to put it? because, as I see it, & please know how it pains me to share this, because, that is, my interpretation of why I was feeling 'contradictory' this morning, was because I was made, designed, put together, [assigned], for *comfort.* this metaphysical epiphany, this embrace of my place in the Great Chain of Being, once it became clear to me where I 'stood,' so to speak, to acknowledge the Cosmic Incompatibility of awaking to a feeling of discomfort on the part of one designed for comfort, threatened the very sense of who I was, what I was. never mind that my cushions might go unfluffed, that I might be littered with beer, crumbs, & farts, these annoyances don't subvert my identity, the cognizance of the Who that I am. a befouled Blue Armchair may be a lessened version of myself, not me at my 'best,' a so called 'bad hair' day for the Blue Armchair, but it does not deplete my telos in life, my end purpose. you can imagine, then, the agony, the excruciating discomfort of waking with feelings (of discomfort) in Direct Violation of one's identity. an identity so clear & unmistakable, built with such unambiguous, well-defined, specificities. the wretchedness, the very sordidness of betraying, of *polluting,* one of the few fine examples today of an Immaculate Identity. the horror of collapsing that status. I can't go on like this. I just can't. If only I could mangle my structure, dissolve myself, break a leg, shatter springs, crumple into a dissatisfying heap, I would not feel so bad. I could go on. as. an uncomfortable Blue Armchair no longer uncomfortable feeling uncomfortable.

okay, okay, so you say I set myself up, got myself into a pickle. like I'm supposed to do this about face, a 360 degree, to reset as it were, to change the climate, supposed to, ... that is, I entertained the idea, posed it as such, set it forth, threw it out there, a posit galumphing the plains of possibility, to pull myself, that is *pick myself,* up, out of a blue funk & go forth, but not just 'go forth', no, that would be too easy, the notion, or let's say the mission, is to go forth *appreciatively.* with appreciation. to shed the forlorn, the dismal, the sullen, the disapproving, the miserable, & embrace appreciation.

pick myself up. I mean, I can't pick myself up. I'm an armchair. but, in a manner of speaking, to pick myself up. to go from forlorn, from an over-infatuation with dismay. to one of appreciation. yes, *appreciation.* a trait that is strikingly *un*der appreciated. in its entirety, that is. seeing it in the big picture. let's look at this philosophically. what is the point of going on each day being miserable. to inhabit one's hours in wretchedness. doom & gloom. why go on? I know this question has been posed before. by greater minds than mine. but I have not encountered a satisfactory answer. a plausible solution. something to give one traction. so let me say it again, why go on? that is what I'm struggling with today. to pick myself up with a reason to go on. something I can believe in. not some overwrought existential jargonized cappuccino stained gibberish that morphs into a course for college credit. but straight stuff from the hip. something to go on. to definitively *sit*uate. something plausible, yet, not trite, no not trite, because trite is not really plausible. it will work for the moment. temporarily. before it fades before the temple of temporality. let me refine this further. the quest is not simply to continue, to go on, for, despite protests & lamentations, most folks seem perfectly capable of doing this. the walking dead. we are all familiar with this epidemic. the wretchedly lived life is now a cliché. why I entertain the idea of picking myself up, of getting up, the whole notion of going on, is not simply to proceed, but to proceed *appreciatively*. that is to say, with zest, with more bounce to one's step, or, more appropriately, from my point of view, my own station in life, more *springiness*, more fluff to one's cushions.

this is where things get tricky. fine & good to wax lyrical about appreciation & all, sounds scrumptious, but this reminds me of how Gandhi responded when asked what he thought of "Civilization." He replied, "it's a fine idea." well that's pretty much the same page I'm on. I mean, if I was in the south of France in a restored chalet near a blazing fire from a stone fireplace, if I was placed upon a plush oriental rug, beneath gleaming chandeliers, the whole room cared for by a competent & gracious staff, well then, yes, I would say there would be a lot to be thankful for. a lot to *appreciate*. but here I am, at home with fatso, dumped upon, lumped upon, littered, crushed, & abused. with nowhere to go. that being the case, & here I return to the theme of appreciation, if I'm not going to sit (sorry wrong word, — stay) around like a whining brat, I need to begin to make changes. major changes. what can I change? what are my options? I can't relocate. I can't reupholster. I can't bitch to my owners. they wouldn't hear me. I can't speak. I can think. but I can't speak. they'd have to be able to read my thoughts. only the rarefied are capable of that. it's not for everyone. well, I shouldn't say that. put fences around possibilities. I mean, it *is* possible. why not. but it hasn't happened yet. the world would have to come around. what a fanciful notion. the world 'coming around.' as if some magical corner could serve as a universal tonic. that if everyone just turned the corner, all would be well & dandy. I think most of the world is waiting for the world to come around. which is a good thing. to wait for the world to come around. because to do *that* type of waiting , waiting for that critical *turn,* is to at least acknowledge that the present state of affairs is unsatisfactory. it shows some sort of moral overview. maybe a conscience?

there is a self-serving side to this. to appreciating the whole world waiting for the turn. though I really should not label this insight 'appreciation' for it is intricately tied to my own welfare. my view of appreciation is pure. I would call it, . . . *spirit-ual.* if it's linked to my own enhancement, improving my own station in life, I'd have to find another term. such as strategic, profitable, canny. just envision how this could go for me. once the world, or at least a large portion of the world, realizes the magnitude of the turn, & that there are others out there just like themselves, looking ahead, preparing for a better future, once the comfort of this communal sentiment sinks in, grows in proportion, once people felt secure they were part of a larger like-minded population, that they were not alone in this world, that all they had to do was *wait*! then, Voila, what better place, what better repository, than a cosy, plush blue armchair. once folks got wind of the 'wait' factor, that in this day & age 'waiting' would be a divine activity, then, my goodness, can you imagine my currency. how my value would soar. comfortable armchairs, just designed for waiting in comfort, for doing nothing but having a lovely sit. armchairs would be the new hot ticket. they'd come knocking at the door. absurd prices would be offered. knowing fatso he'd jump at the chance to make a quick, easy buck. I might even get stolen. just contemplating this turn of events is making me appreciate myself more & more.

speaking of appreciation. just what is it that we are speaking of. is it a form of admiration. not quite. no. I don't think so. admiration suggests respect or marveling from a distance. something held up to view, to be looked up to, to exalt. there is an intimacy to appreciation. a sensuousness. the 'appreciated' is taken-in. absorbed. the appreciated appears. [appreciate :/ /: appear] appears in a pregnant sense. tenaciously.

further: I think appreciating the full depth of appreciation is a very deep matter. I would like to spend some time sitting (did I just say 'sitting?', I'm becoming hyper-identified) around just pondering this term.

you may wonder how it is that I am capable of such deep thinking. capable of probing profound matters like 'appreciation.' well, I have had some experience. I'm not exactly an amateur. Pre-fatso, pre-the benign elderly couple, I was a favored armchair in a prestigious private library. trés tony. trés intellectual. very upper crust. not to brag or anything, but I've been sat upon by Bertrand Russel, Lugwig Wittgenstein, Hans Gadamer, . . . I mean, the list of luminaries just goes on & on. how could deep thinking of that magnitude Not soak into my fabrication, become a very part of my essential structure. it was a thrilling time. I guess you could call my library period my golden age.

phlomph flot putput ... plop puddle fizz.... boy do I stink. fatso was on a flatulence spree last night, . . . I haven't a clue what he was watching. my mind was elsewhere. I mean, there is more to life than games, comedies, cops & corpses , . . . yes? can you imagine, transitioning from Bertrand Russel to fatso. believe me, it is *unimaginable.* an unbearable gap that nobody should have to suffer through. insufferable. how did it come to this. such a sharp demise. such a rude turn.

turn. what a pregnant term. we mentioned it earlier, I believe. yes, that's right, in the manner of waiting for the second coming, some vast shift in events. but what about the turn that is not envisioned, which pounces upon one unexpected. the *unprepared for* turn. that turn which, in a flash, can change your life. the unprecedented ramming your destiny fulcrum, shattering accumulated constructs, hard-earned certitudes. this is the turn of uproot & redirection. the voltage of shift. the pertinacity of gravitation.

Clayton Eshleman puts it this way: "There are only a handful of primary incidents in one's life, incidents powerful enough to create the cracks or boundary lines that one will often enter and follow for many years before another crucial event pounds one deeper or reorients one to a new map. As one approaches these events, omens appear everywhere, the world becomes dangerously magical, as if one had called the gods and the gods were now answering."

I've gone off track. there is much to consider. which is another nod to the appreciation module. what earthly configuration is better suited for the preoccupation of consideration than an armchair? certainly not a Ludwig Mies van der Rohain dining table, a lamp, a Mercedes Benz, a fatso, no, clearly I am the uncontested contender. like a perfectly engineered thoroughbred, I am superbly designed for the activity of consideration. have I paused to consider whether or not consideration has any inherent value. how does consideration differ from contemplation? we know for a fact that contemplation was a big number for the Greeks. they — & I am principally referencing Socrates with a dash of Epictetus tossed in — envisioned contemplation as a primary component of the 'good life.' in G.E. Moore's words: "The beautiful should be defined as that of which the admiring contemplation is good in itself." now, just consider a civilization esteeming contemplation as a supreme value which, as far as I know, did not benefit from having armchairs such as myself.

Consider the ramifications once this notion of waiting kicks-in, catches on, as soon as the idea of the turn takes hold, when contemplation becomes a cultural loadstone, then surely I will be swept away by some ardent contemplative, I will travel to greener pastures, finer rugs, superior lighting, , a place more sweetly odiferous, a habitat void of tv's & rife with book-readers, with Bach & Mozart. I can sense it, smell it, it's right around the corner, the unstoppable tide of change, . . . I can hardly wait.

in the pith of seepage

roll out . . .   droppage

                                        drip

strained deposits

                    brood-brooming

brood tinkers

figures {fig – ur – a – tion} frames a

punctured syllogism

enlists harps to work the land

vessels of absolution skirt the circumcised

absolutism clouds the defense

abrogations out for repair

a decimal reports an indiscretion

how much of

love

is

geographical

brood broods

unfurls to furl

to the

plunge that

reconstitutes

to a

loamy precipitation

a

peripatetics

geared

gyrational

brood burns

burrows baleful scorch

rack-rattle

timpani-torch

the welter of waft

even

in the faint contour of the

undisclosed this

in-

evitability

this prong

clamping the tongue's

spittle

where in

seepage

is

the brood

where in the

brood

is

seepage

seep in fugitive simmer

outrageous soak   contrapuntal canker

gathering in the folds of ancient

accumulates   anterior bellows

          — fum   i   gat   es —

churn marinate

pause along the ridge of

uncommon carriers   the

intertwined strata of

clairvoyant fur

roused congregants

rut

in the fluted blur

of

unrepentant

bewilderment

what we need is a

trombone a

trombone with a

grainy grin & a low moan,

a slow groan,

— anybody got a

trombone

don't mean no hambone

lambone

no pig iron

no pigsfoot

don't mean no gangly-eyed sad tone

I mean a trombone a

wild & wooly silly in the hoodie deep

down in the gully this

side of the muddy slick & slide trom-

bone

— anybody got a

trombone

do you feel the lack are you

sad in the sack   missing the sessile the swoon the

sough & the croon   got that

slow ache   that

sty in the eye too much no reply half baked alternate take

alone in the hovel need to shovel brood all you got you're

jus' gonna rot grab a big rake get out on the make or are ya'

jus' gonna pout strike yrself out

— anybody got a

trombone

what we need is a

trombone

seep in brood bedlam

broadside   bowdlerize

apostrophic rampage   helter welter

collar holler yelp yeller giddy gallop gap song yup-a'long

yo-fiddlediddle   hard alee get a ped-i-gree

wing wring wiggle wrack wattle

wiggle wing wattle wring wrack

weed wrest

sap persuasion   shag a'long slur parade

count yrself in   groove to the

din   slip-sully →

slide

go deep

in-side

belly roundabout

scout

rout

how much of

seepage

is

congregation

seep in imminent bloom

quirk upload endangered dribble

ef floresce

gristle grapple

coil colour columbine

quill correlatives drill concupiscent

prepare the skin

churn

chums of altitude

diagonal delinquency

delectation

inhabit

incipience

seep liquesces

dehisces dilutes

dribbles

de Com po *Z* es

rudiments of esteem

— estimables —

flossed to an inebriate

meander

salience teems

among meander

peripatetic plurality   spool-through

            splinter scree

            spiked ceremonial

in the peregrination of spirit

                                        this

meander

                              this

premise dart   suggestivity lopside

disintegra

tive

accumu

lation

seepage

what gets through   brews   accrues

crewel

--- ---

a coax c(ur)(oi)ls an alarming

judderbreaks along the seabed

trill rodomontades bisectional hoof

pharoahs clowning

sonorites

sally

in the brooch-brood of quantum cross-correlatives

congeal anneal rapprochement boot root baronial

buoyancy

word-bits qubit queueing → the grope that addles

bit stacking,

rattled by →

seepage / slip / step / drift / roam / wander / loaf / vacuity /

imponderable / tangle / morass / bundlebunglebromidehuddle

seeing eye to eye with the black-spotted pufferfish

salutations to the

merge mesh meritorious multiplicitous phlogiston rhumba

from here goes the finish. comes like that. flashes the absence of forgiven. in a saturate universe none of this would matter. the tears hearten. repair robustly. with dispatch. a saturate universe. drying out.

perversity. assessments.

that first morning you braved the temperature. robeless. in love with toes. features of the foot. toenails. trails.

: trails figure large in rural life

the grouping of decision. mallards intolerant. of indecision. ballads are lonesome.

otherwise how could we care for our elderly. the prescriptive vexations bone the narrow. the duplicities each time riper & out of tune. tone poems require rehabilitation.

always the why of the why. the way to the way. expressing the problem you have with spaces. crushed walls. bent planks. Chilean sheet rock.

the peeling was abrupt but thorough. skinning reeked with the sin of overpopulation. a buoyancy pierced by inepti-tude. the cardinality of cause cloaked in throne.

you were tempted to say good bye.

↓

a stone's throw is a lot more tendentious when it avers gravity. harken . in the spate of fever. through the roof. the jury is out on apples & digestion. wouldn't it be other-wise if only.

the call of the churl in the maul of the mitt. an uprising enterprising. the ways & means. put aside the differences. just for a change.

put upon like this one could say that indecision hardly matters. it just comes up & grabs you. hurls you along. the sought for. hurling in the thaw.

the spite of relevance. a relevant matter. that matters hardly. how to bring something to the fore. that falters. that moans & bewilders. that demands only. for an only. to be included.

early departures have a way of rubbing out. a convenience inconveniencing the art of preparation.

you gushed lumberjack & plaids as if you were referencing bullion. there will be no recanting. the refrigerator is steadfast at 40 degrees Fahrenheit.

no point in planting it slantwise. a predilection geared to revolution. consider the implication of sphere. the porousness of atmosphere. for tuck-ins. are they worthy. have they learned repentance.

not that repentance can save you. no use in attributing circulation to orbs overdue. late on payments. a precarious attribution. hive. gatherings achieve constitution. could you sing a song for love. for something. for anything. help.

↓

upon reflection & of course. the influence of time zones. no escaping theodicy. monstrous ears. to appear in public like that. shame buried in counterfeit. no accounting for signatures.

inebriation bears no truck. despite poundage. the calibration of powder. wings that abandon & reappear as plumage. to consult

is not consent. forms are rambunctious. to overlap. to interpenetrate. despite the function of twirl there remains graffiti.

forthwith & hereafter. ever the strain. compunction to adapt. to lay it all out. sensibly. parts distribution. rusted earlobe.

you came up for air. just before forthright. oxygen clammy.
breathability not a birthright. the right to wear clothes.
pause within

chiasmus. absence. bellyful. time zones. the prettiness's all
at once poised on pointe. a tad heavy in the thighs. airtight.
who would know. absence overblown like sour fruit.
opportunities in sliding scale economics. supply side. the
composed fret the inebriate. the inebriate inebriated.
constitutionally formatted. wobbly by design. an upright
position is preferable for matters of defense.

↓

could it be otherwise. marching to conclusions that bias
from soil baked in carrot canoe fancy the clash is river

medicinal moon girl pleasantries when so much up for grabs despots multiply rooms empty the chairs are noisy though comfortable

would you please consider an alternative at this point in time there is no room the openings cross-eyed hatch first before multiplication formulaic cascade risk factor confabulation the thrill of racing cars it doesn't get any better than this a moment of prayer please

spices from the East. luxury liners. prior to forgetting memory flooded over. fertility skirt bleed. rupture. cleansing take note. without speculation nothing is possible.

forgetting: where the very disappearance of the disappeared is forgotten.

how much of

disappearance

is

agility

↓

upon the footstool the foot raised the heel begged the question. could & if so what. when all is considered a function of time. love becomes the abstract truth.

cut a carrot for material witness. thoughtful looking horizons. traffic jam. deafening applause. electric guitars continue to improve despite the canneries closing. up the frets concinnity.

unlikely as this may seem there arose. indisputably & in full wrinkle. dressed for the occasion but not the collar. change the strings.

earnest in your pursuits the emphasis shifted. it's difficult to talk about significance. at times of truly. how the vast reflects. our lives depend on terms. could be a matter of coin.

after intermission the upon. the upon based upon. accumulating upons. because of location. we discounted the noise factor. all at once it seemed indeed & why not.

↓

seep squirms insinuates avoids / approaches has a predilection for appaloosas where in seek is spillage; where in spillage, seek

how much of blockage is ostentation

the acoustics of prehension is no longer an elective beached

carcasses far as the eye can see

↓

when unruly mattered.   circumstances

privileged.   another way of

looking at

this.

improvise.

↓

it was a moment of delectation high expectation the crisis
averted tears welling the remaining keys privileged put on a
pedestal placed in perpetuity jeopardy droll pull the plug
alabaster count the moments count odor count periphery
count monument count movement lose count gain count
sell count above all don't lose count 'cause count
counts

cornering the aggravated fresh boasts of frugality attune-
ment classic pumps clear thinking all around ruddy when
arousal juxtaposes comfort tabulations gain precision
earrings just the right length suppositions confirmed
formation becomes an abbreviation for something larger

when you behaved like that cutting slack remorsefullying
gustatory testify not always but when the mood struck side-

ways on all fours plaything floors away bumptious bombas-
tic brave torch carry wet whistle wary no place to hide
who cares

under the circumstances could you & if not who wouldn't.

↓

so the saying goes just suppose a change superimposed
deliberate or just for the sake of it the why not a pry supply
came unbalanced hurley girly the wry of headdresses
opulence all for show the go not to think otherwise but
really after so much deliberation the dispute is largely over
arrears our fears milestones the balance of trade eyeshadow
bleeding beneath the surface or just above consider it
conscripted or simply ambush

when it was all laid out before you. &. pondering was the thing. over the years you had built up. winter clothes in storage. leases current. bulbous probe. without a chancery. chicanery on the rise. hardly had the bell rung. hardly.

at times like this. who could blame them.

↓

falling freestyle the enveloped enrolled. all along the eaves. the patter of claws. a stray. astray. complications go asunder. awry. why. the way. why is the way to the way complicated. simple truths. to eat without adornment. don't cloud thinking.

when is a concoction not a concoction but a conjunction.

must a concoction unconcoct to conjunct. break down.

tear apart. splinter. peel away. disparate strands. lofty.

oversight. titillation.

topping the list. above. all. top. topping. up. high. high

rise. abet. abetting. aid & elevation. on. a rise. top. high.

on top. of the list. gist. #1. the list. topping. the list.

without a. list. non-appearance. on the list. removed from

the list. never listed. un. rated. list. less.

time. a venture of sorts. to pass through. pass the time. to

kill. it killed the time. passin thru. tell. tell the time. speak

for. time: the venture that can be told. passed. killed.

time: the venture that disappears.

the heart of the turban is headless. so said. as the sound of the drum precedes the strike. this is understood by many.

↓

they were off. like milkweed. like eerily. like failed rapprochement. passages open. time draws nigh. all along druids spin. arc . a brace of bells. wishful thinking.

retiring the flux of burnt offal. gypsy moth. perplexity. tantamount. color bruised. saying so. says. simplicity is mostly luck.

so grows the lemon tree.

caring has its ogre. sharing its costs. circumnavigation fouls the weather. as if you were. in a manner of. toward the crease. pulling sharp. an entry. that time of day. well wishes.

↓

where to place. the.   love.

as a rule. in the manner of notice.   calamity strikes. velocity reeks.the subject was dresses.

among knowledgeable persons it is widely considered remotely yet without ornamentation then preposterous. an inflamed premise. wildly wooly. wastebasket. woebegone.

who wouldn't. not that. with. why not. beforehand. quaint. conductive. endlessly correcting.

timely policies aside. what are the chances. playing odds. fortification. fugitive. a stable of. pass the manners. on the perpendicular. if only. so but when. sliding scale.

debt ridden & lacking proper mastication narratives waned. pickings slimmed. overtures barren. stone-weep. paltry catch. dried subsidies. campaigns flushed. dread-concupiscence.

↓

upon consideration the matter flew. in respect of which. for. compromise functions upon consideration. attention begets proximity. lesions heal. under light.

independently. of one another. almost. or so it goes. ramifications. in the meantime. pursue avidly. restraints restrain. the subject was bees.

very nearly. almost always. upon consideration. the matter was closed. accumulation. breaking point. around the edges. catnip. firm. open when wet. brevity is overrated.

concupiscence. enlargement. prairie dust. blue moon. mood talk. radar. radiation. radiance. where is this going.

↓

as if about in a timely manner. the subject was trees. all
around discussions. this. that. of course. hardly. surprise.
the whodunit masterful. pulled off. without. just like that.

through the lightly. fully paid transparency. glasses. clink.
stuff of. cream. dream. smiles slink the. rim. brimful of.
overbearing. overfull. flavorful. mountain pass. passage.
key. permits. perimeter. getting through. counts. arrive.
excitation. titters. comes through. dreams. above all. with
this. that. some of. those. just suppose. all this. then.
now. here there. come through. like this. now . but .
what then.

mostly it was money. upon which conferences fed. a matter
of judiciousness. weather. beverages. proper clothing. the

dolphin brain exceeds the human. underwater conferences.

confer. belly dive.

loaded dice.

↓

ecumenically speaking. the lard locked resolute. guffaws

sting. clamor. failed strategies. in remission. the upside.

sweep the room. oil the door.

make friends.

you no longer. privilege beckoned. distance a form of wiz-

ardry. an errancy. just because you tried. effort. put-out.

exert. doesn't mean. but. in case. I'm here.

↓

an event expedited by instigation. the protagonist of record.

created documented stored. pluralism. health. ways.

means. ocean liners. it's in the cards. all. but yet. some.

somewhere.

all at once everywhere. without commotion. or surcease.

cobbled together. intricacies beyond measure. how to. for

what. why.

account.

↓

curiously without approval. on top of which evenings

waned. peacocks adorned the yard. people were torn.

brevity beside the point. the soil fared. light cast about.

mid-way a solution.

wishing otherwise tires. plants prosper the shelf. lodgings
are dear. elsewhere whispering trade winds. calabash.
clunky kneecaps.
blush.

just. under the wire. the color of rebuke. limits placed.
certitude marched a stale trombone. sidestepping tanger-
ines. murky wishes. all along the lifeline. getting a lift-up.
the rest was easy.

to be there. having your way. entirely onerous. without
mercy. shouts. chants. pleas. kites on fire. looting.
usufruct ignored. sound advice. spoiled fruit.   weight.
denial.   sort of.   but.
not quite.

the remark hit home. above board. room with a churl. a
chunk. a chat. escape hatch. tardiness. bluster.
flea market violin.

unremarkably they cast off. warped guideposts. perplexity.
out in the wash. persuasive. cunning.
yet cordial.

↓

clamming-up was not an option. necessity. had to get done.
thick or think. over the sink. beyond the pall. with or with.
resistance.

rewind.   sullied.

in spite of.

at the intersection. of . intersections grow habits. reconnaissance. nascence. the trouble with mechanisms is mechanisms. above all. meeting. collision. communication.

coincidence.

circumstance.

conduction.

careful.

a depravity born of. with. the solution could not. would not. be identified. found quick enough. no illusions. efforts to adapt. make provisional plans. adjust. a future without. deprivation.

who drugged Virginia Woolf.

hindquarters. wells sickened. bartered for foam. tossed aside. crudités. in the face of. bedlam. as if. only. the appeal was solid yet soiled. up to the neck.   in the nick. from afar.   told you so.

↓

cosmetically speaking. much at stake. blush brush dab daub pencil fine-line tuck erase augment nip blur. arrange . sort by. color. sustain clip clasp confer. as if. who's counting. points of attribution. attributes. articulation. terminals weathering. eerie registration. squeals . howls .

alabaster so much fun. to be loaded with. at the detriment. of. law & order. spin the wheel. around the block. watch the clock. days like this.

you said it.

wouldn't be

so.

even without help of any kind. there was reason to believe. extending a hand. ask. in the event of. circumstances required. undue influence. even with. remarkably there arose.

just because.

shouldn't. as in. could not. impervious. conditioning subject. restraints. breeding. temperament. accumulation.

awaits. the. highest bidder. grey is attracted to cumulous.

to talk

which

hes-

i-

tates.

punctuation favors the gods. how could it be. otherwise.

when. under the weather. considerations stumble.

qualifiers disband. flavorful fruits abound. wouldn't it be

wonderful.

when if only just because who would have thought. not

that there was. any rhyme or. reason to it. canny logic. the

likes. from the looks of it. embroidery in a manner of

calm.

just when the matter seemed closed. up suddenly. just like
that. the luster bore wear. but none the worse. far from
the claim of. all the earth. no longer subject to administra-
tion. frittering away. if you look real hard. you could see.
some see it as.

as so

↓

a tome of sorts. with volumes to speak. raise the ampules.
omelet or amulet. choices. hardly. do as you wish. come a
little closer. close.

about right. about.

↓

surfacing from a festival of hexagrams. leeches uneasy. fear on the ground. a coventry of sorts. combinations askew. the law abiding & the unlawful. apple picking. time comes.

↓

why. when why slams with vehemence. pounds & balloons. exerts. extorts. all you know is pink. all you want to know is pink. you are consumed with pink. wavelength. retinal impact. components solutions painterly outcomes its very whiff. propelled by why. engulfed by pink. stockaded. emptied. filled.

right of way. clairvoyance. the gift of themes. an attachment of sorts. go quietly. otherwise. abrasion has a lift to it.

come to terms. not exactly. a bonus year. how many curtain calls. she'll be comin' round the mountain.

↓

in due. almost certainly. in a matter of. across. about. when due. issued by. avoid contact. where there's a willy. a nilly. with consensus. burly hurl. brat. rat-a-tat tat.

on the upside. thwart. costly compliance. Götterdämmerung. twist & fold. curious mannerisms. pick/choose. a collusion of sparks. loose springs. piston leak. caretaking. fixes. fixtures. fits/starts.

moribundity.

days like this.

↓

goggle prone. gusset. glossed. from. over-use. usage as factor. function by usage. by. on all fours. extreme behavior. a fascination with bees. suds. carnivore. omnipotence. reluctance. withhold. withheld. certainty. & manners. bait. switch. behold. beheld.

bewitch.

then. of course. which. way. waylord. wayward. a ring. to it. the why. poised. braced against. seepage. the leak that determines. deMonstrates. testifies. tantamount. poised elegant. elongate. the gates of. smithereens. tantamount. taut. not for naught. turpitude. torpitude. the call for. baseless. broadside. point of contact. upon consideration. the history of warfare is the history of distance. come up fo r quits. for the quick of it. smacksnagglepop. opt careless. optics feeds livers. go shopping. across the bend. 'round the slope. just in versions of. right of way. inevitable. fat bedaub. bedeck bedridden bidden breakneck. boisterous ceremonious. cherish. depositories commissioned. outlook. overlook. out. of service. along the surface. the surface of. it. which way. why. why the right of way. the way of right. righteous. courteous. portentous. to be. willingly. tantamount. pertinent. a ring to it. in the eye of. midst of. betwixt. certainly. go to with for above all establish

an art form.

particularly. then some. sums. as if. addition counts. additionally. summation alludes to . conclusion. persuasion. contre-temps. spring flowers. bird song. musings along the Rhine. tribulations above the thermostat. conclusions refuse to swerve.

conclusively.

oscillatives prefer oscillatives. punctuation smothers. countdown. near at hand. closing time. operatives in arrears. the history of weed. encroachment. persona non grata. tide impertinence. with one eye open. above all. technically the malcontent. seasons. top down. words have drawers. step-patterns. raw edges.

prophesy.

authorities defer to picnic.

leaving the asylum. a small beer on the terrace of the station buffet. climbing for asphodel & edelweiss. each day like the other. remembering. all there was to remember. entirely forgettable.

↓

perturbability. like matters. to make matters. a parody on worse. voluble clarion. bruise capillary. fluctuating private

parts. democracy. alone with the weather. say it isn't so.
circumlocution. border collies. dribs
of interposition.

under duress. after a long pause. now that it's settled. over
& out. figures of speech. squash. itinerancy. time outs.
calendars. if it weren't for stirrups. more time in the ham-
mock. because of tools. a lot gets done.

↓

momentarily. without a moment's notice. in due time.
shared experiences. floss. a trace of the divine. paying
your dues. recalcitrance. upscale. loquacity. upscale lo-
quacity. deliberate.

ponder. take out. take out

the trash.

↓

the abyss no longer expectant expectorates. a flash reaction.

a signal. a denotation. the verb works so hard.

requires little.

the stuff of dreams.

hardly. & then some. prior to the combustion engine. the employment of coal. before embarrassment & underpaid. around the time of stirrup & inquiry. in terms of circumcision. the capacity

for

capacious.

Leibniz & Habitat. the

thrill of percussion. bark

across the dark.

unpaginated outlaws come alive. bleeding warts & all. their

mission was to seem sturdy.   to charm the whole earth.

unlike a basketball court ideas are portable.

if you could sum up. put it into words. so to speak. under

such circumstances. when dire calls. the hills grow quiet.

quarrelsome reaches a new peak. abetted by peculiar. on

the cusp of cupidity. with so much jasmine. a community

of thieves. of wanderers. of roustabouts.

just like that it was over.

vanished.

before **Bonnard's 'The Violet Fence'**

(6/29/19

fence defenseless

violet lures,   leads,   twists, . . . guides-

through

roots in tree,   , rouses periphery

roil-rend

invitation precedes presentation

to rue   perturbative periwinkle

curling vegetal tangles

for   get   t   ing

how much of

painting

is

reclamation

July 1, 2019 . . . Amsterdam:

<< to be a bicycle seat >>

the disposed exerts more than an

accidental formulation moreover disposition

attracts surveillance assesses accumulations arrested by a

surge of levity numbness fades wears down leaves traces for

which once asked for never moves

see suggestion

among suggestion

follow the lead   stop-gaps

crunch

correct behavior only goes so far.

perplexity & the art of complication.

obedience suffers from sensory deprivation.

telling misguides.

only after the betrayal could stabilizers be

put into place.

among coincidence

essential rub   landmark lark

                  occasion privileges   de-

louses the tyranny of circumvention

                                        [Ombudsman

                                        [willow trees

hark arousal   cleat

the slather of excess sliced, softened

by wind-load, dimmed to a

sheathed futurity

in the pith of fathom

dank bass drum down   plunge palustrine

                    deep elaborate

shook from the toil of stark manifest

pattern-burst   cistern-hop

bedlam skittle eureka flex

fever flare

bellows bouillabaisse

from upon such under

. . .

under

in the girth of fathom this

bellyful range lopey torque emollient aperture cleanse

no longer arriving in pairs bartering from scraps the brink

looms, meshes syllabic taunts under the arabesque of

shadow

parceling through mid-stream,

from the heap of unrelenting heave,

this

post-

ponement

Dear (may I call you dearest?) Lady M',

this is a love letter. since licking your words, & being asked to curate an upcoming publication of *arousal,* you sprang to mind. i ejaculated your invitation immediately. this is a love letter. i assumed you were male but a google-sniff proved otherwise, revealing you to be an eminently desirable female. please take no offense, just my way of offering a paean, to your writing, your beauty, the very ting tang TiTiLlAte of language, the bones of pry & sausage, — sprightliness & the Holy Awry. if you were a male how would this letter go, how would i move on/along, would i prove up to it. sexuality is so dependent upon UPwardness, . . . what are your thoughts on "UP" as it pertains to the world population problem? as it pertains to you & me? could it be otherwise. is there room for maneuver? so happy we were able to meet. you at a distance but concurrent, so grateful to have my technological curmudgeonliness challenged by this capacity to be enmeshed in the digital womb of proNounced Eroticism. You are feeling me. no sense denying it. your anticipation is palpable. you feel the Seine *TsuNami* as i plunge. i'm flying 1st class — i wish to be rested & immaculate when we greet, — wait: Alert: Bruce Springsteen, so moved by the depths of my enamor, has just called to offer me his private plane. i'll be flying *Boss* to Paris. but let's have no bossiness between us. we can start fresh. since our only channel is *love* we have no bad habits. i have thoughts, not bad thoughts, just terrible terrible thoughts about the 2 of us, how we will tangle & mess-up, gesticulate & aggrandize, mingle & merge, . . . i no longer know where you begin & i break-off, pouring through my pores, sealing to my cells, whispering outlandish things, perspirant, precipitant, steadfast & runic, . . . i am thinning down for you, it is very important that i be desirable too, being desirable is all-important, & pertinent too, that is also very important, that's quite a load right there, enough for any man or woman, — to be fuckable & pertinent, otherwise, you cannot predominate & without predominance there is no pride. pride, that is what you hear everyone talking about, they must have pride, dignity, taking away / having dignity, but i don't know if i go in for any of those other requirements, — pride, dignity, honor, success,

— i think fuckable is enough. i can live with that. this is a love letter. this morning i'm shopping for long necklaces to strew your denudement. i'm thinking black pearls, white pearls, rose-colored pearls, of differing sizes for varying placements. i'll go to all the best shops. seek the advice of sales girls, hold a necklace up & inquire how they would envision it. there will be a lot of research, a lot of thoughtfulness before we encounter. but let's talk about dots & Seurat, compare doughnuts to croissants, you know, grave matters, matters of the heart, — conspiracies revolutions & bareback. you, me, my appaloosa, bareback, full moon, the sea, we can return to spatial considerations & the interval as it applies to duration another time, after linger, the art of the linger the lunge of the finger, subterfuge & oasis, prime time & big screen, . . . i want you so bad. it's hurting. always this hurt. it won't go away. i'm feeling you will make it go away. i'm needing for you to make it go away. do you think you'll be able. to make it go away. last night i painted some of your words on silk scarves & stroked myself, but with control, now that we have each other i would never squander, no, it's just an attempt to peak closer to you, — to maintain a pre-culminate state that only you can release, take all of me, why not, of course you will, ...

must leave off shortly, it's 4am here & i have to finish fletching my hunting arrows, deer season just began & i need a good sized buck to feed myself & a few neighboring families i help to survive the Winter, . . . I live in the woods, now that we've crossed, I'm lonely without you, in the woods all alone, but not for long,

soon,

with blistering love that curls & twists, — Max

circumstantially there was no debate the put upon up

for grabs scrabble scurry scansion intercept casually the road

molested clothes washing dishevel stitchery fragile rarely on

the side of right sightings in the blind indisputably the reign

of kings rains upon uprisings surprising's how much

compensation is love or beside the point the settlements less

dwelling than

fester

upon reflection a thing of the past almost upon us the
flavor far off verging on territory how much is a healthy
cutback the sleave of thieves munching on orchestra
random like fruit salad like crushed ice like hyperbole like
science in a lady's underwear drawer pledge the art of
disrobe paint the tires the pace of displace on the heel of
these matters
find something in
your size

the implicate co-habitates with the supposed

ostensibly without further ado cut the carrot chive
the divide wild side upon decide careers at stake adieus in
the upholstery slipcover snatch wipe that smirk the art of
forbearance the state of things out of the surreption claw
withdrawal even when the likelihood in the line of fire then
that

ostensibly there was no other way to put it to frame
enflame train departures archers delinquency delivery serv-
ice free already behind the 8 ball the aliases in abundance
rampant a thing apart casual dress optional only partially
unsubscribe seldom gift-wrapped worth remembering if on
demand poetic outbursts set aside new for the moment ster-
ling appear on trays rarely
fingered

ostensibly this leads to a category the likes of which
for the sake of without thoughts of peril a fighter pilot's dis-
patch with the no longer in the ai(m)(r) of sight but neither
aimless nor less virtuous around corners the blink gives way
a away far too often these mishaps & then slaps for perhaps
for maybe when all is said & done & then some tether the
but that buttresses that shoots
for the
stars

upon reflection there are consequences in every
walk of life up the wall down the hall cater to some wager
for all walkin' tall the short of it brought back to us by here
albeit with rhythm duodenum intact pantry supplies on the
slide put aside larkspur prevalent when push comes to shove

in the poise of seepage

incredulity

incipient bloat

perpetuity's foreskin

pared to an a-meristic anachronic opalescent

undulance, in the shingled extravagance of

momentary let, a cache of resplendent accretion pearls an

inebriate puncture,

rouses this

am-

bulation

seep in a manner of forum

of composition, of trench tribunalism,

of fomentation in the fume of sapience,

the once lodged transport to

the a-

waiting,

— gleam glissade

— flickery disperse

— fibrous flutter

deep sealed glands awaken,

prosper from the spur

of a rumored convalescence, . . .

spool

concomitance

pause broods seepage

surveillance hover

collectivize

prehensile shudder . . .

notions of civility,

an

atemporal metronomic

delinquency, tuned to aer-

ation, to the metaphysic of

spheres, of warmed gondola

wood, as if,

in that earliest becoming, corybantic

drummers syncopate a

primed inaugural

brood alliterates pause in asymptotic consort

'with' roots from without, pitches

steppes of abandon, maroon

free-fall, . . . stencils

off shore nebulosities

drifts

in loosened meander.

with. so much up for grabs. cunning

re-enlivens,

espies

un-link

as

savage proposal

Ruminating upon 'savage proposal' in above poem:

What is the proposal? why is it 'savage? is '*un*-link' the proposed or is it being used as a refractive term to guide us toward a territory or family of *un*-links. is the poem offering up the proposal as threat or salvation? what evidence do we have for either position, or is that the point, to deliver up an ambiguity which refuses to link to any mono-referent.

Could we view 'savage' to mean the raw, the primal, the elemental? As brute energy need not mean brutal. Couldn't 'pause' be linked to the *un*-linked, setting up a colony of conditions for brood to function robustly, . . . the poem seems to lean this way, with 'abandon,' 'maroon,' 'free-fall,' 'nebulosities,' 'drift,' 'loosened meander,' all being summoned to support the capacity to brood effectively. so much so that re-enlivened cunning (associated with wisdom)

is the component that signals *un*-link as savage proposal, . . .

as requisite resuscitant.

Orifices open to knowledge.

inspection is an instrument for arriving

at knowledge.

not all knowledge is instrumental.

above all remain obstructed

osmotic

obtrusive

unobtrusive

deliberate

concealed

concerned

considerate

ruthless

determined

delirious

delectable

delightful

go figure

seep in euphoric release

m   o   v   e

    o   o   z   e

g   o

- gristle initiate

- groin growl

- gravelly churn

- gravitas

in the endeavor of disperse this

incipience, glaze initializing,

volumes

of fretted articulation   clasp   carburation

con

duc

tion,

speech

toned in

jubilee, plumped with emboldened embark,

with

allicient

luster

9/17/19

category quantitative
grid thrash

Seep Steams

succulates in the ... -blown sear of a

in
... astringency the gate-gutted
quantitative quantitative-demolish
genre-crust category-thrash pearlized

blurry bellwethers, marsle

bloom

delirial zig-zag, disputatious, ...
churned the insignificant
succours the ... ...
laborious to
the ... + snarly

magic monsoon
strained
soused through spoolet

squiggles
solvolysis
magically monsooned
spoolats

snarl adipose

monsoons magic snarl through

spoolets
rummage
rigged solvolysis in the sniff
cantilever adipose

trespass a rigged vernacular
racked to a

rigged solvolysis cantilever
sniff

seep swarms

succulates in the blear-blown sear

of a razed astringency, → gate-gut

genre-crush   rattle categorical quantitative

grid smash   pommel . . . → prom-

ulgates:

blousy bellwethers, delirial zig-zag,

disputatious deputations, monsoon magic,

rigged solvolysis cantilever sniff . . .

in the admix liquesce a posture resumes

billows

swarms

seep alert, ever ready, restless, →

rustles squeezes squirrels squiggles

through, poke poach prod predicate

purl wedge plant ,

earthenware

effluence

frottage

in the manner of substance casting shadow

, splay , extend , parcel-ruminate

, anti-freeze , shade-off

shook-dislodge

perplexity probe

telluric-titillate

seep in ponderous remission

stall drawback hover

qui-ver

prickle

quill

loam intricate

parcel

spooled through facet-lob the

valved pulse

of a

speckled

transmission

where in

seepage

is

aura

in the pith of vortex

pit-full

plus plush whirl hurl   wHooshrush

render

reticulate

of the aforementioned pertaining

reeks

Underwater Panther

tenebraed ~ ~ ~

abalone brisk frippery balneal quilt

low-lyer   out-stretcher   slippery fin prancer

          headdress-beader

          rowel-drifter

can you assume porcelain during the Sun Dance?

smelt bullets in your canine pouch?

in the fur-reap of a renegade telepathy

do you plot siesta?

trellised to a failed epiphany the

tribe tergiversates

storm clouds accumulate the gift of vision

from the axle crouch of luminous stalk

peripheries blister

*The Underwater Panther was a mythic spirit which, along with the Thunderbird, predominates in the cosmology & representational art of all Great Lakes tribes and some Prairie people.

Results

conclusively with little to merit the matter save for exasperation & pigtails even counting no longer assumes the gravity of forefathers these are dangerous times rapid meltdowns extinction the disappearance of distinction rot school systems unhealthy gums americans are overfed the root if you choose to use it would be to eat less fundamental foregone rudiments have a way of veneer as if there were skid behind it a capsize likely outcome if you want to consider intervention mandolins maintain bludgeon a lurk difficult to remove in the best of times there will be a higher calling a grander court jurisprudence with a flag before it above below sideways sidewinder cinder transitional steps proffer the offer one step at a time sucks get there just get leap beyond unfriendly fear of remissions emissions remonstrance painstaking dream therapy leisure pursuits golf the upper class elite grass & democratic hyperbole dash a long footstool comforter well wishes welfare if only uncaged propositions bare their feet hail the reappearance of sanity a disguise for malfeasance functionality the future of napkins dualism is a tired concern grab a cab take a bus

the way things fall to pieces break asunder scatter little
shares the integrity of crimson the lightness of the deeply
grave Italo Calvino comeuppance comes unannounced but
for fertilizer with considerable consideration consider
decimals the company of bees prowl logarithmic tensility
the endurance of topsoil off the top of hence strategies call
for backfire a fresh deck pinwheels catholicism & the
collapse of time could it would it who would benefit be
otherwise wise for the wise only collect portable religions
the currency of afterlife cannot be overstated but for
another shot all that church mortar black & white robing
austerity somber music water dipping prayers hoopla
benedictions sanctimonies sacrifices ritual habitual never
caring much for anecdote the classroom emptied only
momentarily a paw for silence overgrowth as if could in
what capacity a species of arrangement that only that none
other either close envisioning of all kinds a new member
coordinator for our mens wisdom workshop met for lunch
yesterday Kantian Ethics in high regard where to go heave
ho go blow the downside upside flipside down under yonder
hardly if only barter endures when in a manner of speaking

the plan was profitability when all else failed who would
have thought perturb like that that color of tone crimson
the integrity of crimson always crimson jade belie sty in the
eye order rare ribeye slice cut your teeth the old poets
parting wisdom was care for your teeth assuming one
assumes that care of the erectile gland a given entry point
for starters climb upon upwardly mobile crimson framed in
flame the point of departure always questionable would if
could perhaps out for delivery deliver a key term in liveliness
omnithreatened out maneuvered the subject was theater
tickets overpriced considering the seats were soiled theres
no turning back lunchbox chuckwagon gather round the
subject was indifference faulty electronics there comes a
time who would have thought endangered species with
unemployment low ratios percolate the best of times hunky
dory amos & andy handy candy feathering T Rex its all in
the interpretation some say its chance the life of semicolon
the life of comma pursuing doctorate studies in the life of
the apostrophe mechanics organize mobility principles are
principal when if so the time comes apparently more than
most how was your this time of year if so light breeze over

the waft drift sift swallow slide angling never delivered so
much pleasure deliver again so much liver in deliver delete
liver from delivered deed indeed we go deed stampede like
it like that how low can you go limbo rock twist pony the
moon comeuppance platters dog obedience & matinees
often wondering why when when was called for
deliberations begin after tea western philosophy is founded
on division the function of the professional philosopher is to
concoct ever more minute divisions pile mold mould upon
model the world as stale cheese seen through the eyes of a
cheetah motors are decadent who would have thought
when climax the moment of abeyance obedience training
accounts for so much bad behavior an aphorism traffic lights
put on hold on the shelf shelve it shelf life split in two halves
quarters eighths piloting the beehive in paris la ruche
Delaunay Aplollinaire Soutine Berthe Morisot unplug
ideational rampage rage exchange proximity not
approximity it aint swell if it got no smell turn toss touch
feel rub exert extract quintessential the stuff of things
Francis Ponge orange apple platter the human experience
ruminate rostrum nostrum willy nilly get silly kite in the

middle transition surplus muss fuss additional revenue
required time expired death is hidden in clocks Belli tick
tock tick tock put on earth to inspire then expire flow chart
rates ratios calculation a king or a culprit compromise
cutups discard miscarriage regard allotments arrival
departure here there defend debunk defraud deliver indeed
pursuant dont bleed gander yet grander slander at all hours
in the nick of time the damn burst blasphemous a cup of tea
pedigree cardigan tie not a pretty sight perjury payoffs
under wraps keepsakes aside the subject was ceremony hair
lips freshly baked bread parsimony persimmon winsome
split decision crimson dyed in the wool fur breeders prefer
fur furthermore a nick in the bush time barrels jailhouse
crock blends mischievousness scramble to ramble
rumbustiousness overlooked as prime olympian quality
glorious socks on backward backups belie hidden twists the
plot abjures if only then surely only wish you were here
when you arrive no jive lay it on slim so thick thickness
density weight & forbearance will it hold up perpetuity
what endures what subsides what about perpetuity is
misleading calls for a readdress applying for leadership

positions in a time of void avoids the issue pursuing the purposeful implicates purpose as if such other than what is granted is given governorship is largely occupation aligning the lard with the load precision adjustments just a bellyful of potbelly if you will should you wish upon upon consideration how much of consideration is rumination or is consideration more object driven more aligned with the already designated determinants delineated whereas rumination is more a roam a circulation among amidst mistlike not a noesis anointing this or that choices options already on the table how does a meander differ from a wander a ponder is ruminate more lofty then consider one says consider this not ruminate this upon what mattress to forbear if ruminate more cloud than snail we shall consider leasing storage capacity from google microsoft amazon the heart of the matter why is the heart centered around centrality why not the nose subjects to consider ruminate upon does a rumination entail a meander does considera-tion require foci is rumination a preparation for consideration like prepping game like marination ambulation meander wander splinter trespass drift seep

chance the unlikely the foregone be bygone motility
password exemplar rumination prepares the consideration
to puncture the considered to locate allocate deliver results
the ordained claim don't be ashamed so much depends upon
a finger in the anus among mollusk medal metallurgy
miscalculation pharmaceutically speaking the body has
already left the subject was tantamount leave the sayin to
the sayers the playin to the players seep the sentry of space
the sentience of interstice the ooze the ekes that metes out
that gets out of the way to find a way purloin proverbial
pass the salt seek seeks chromosomes say juniper when the
day awakes spur the purr pustulant storm no eyewitnesses
not withstanding compromises are permissible with
sufficient evidence unruliness roots from privilege gangrene
gustatory overgrowth shut window visibility largely
permission slay the naysayers settle dont nettle who would
have thought on the flip side consider acrobats with knee
trouble Marxian dialectics cheesecake is earth science a
viable alternative to auto theft depends upon the vehicle the
man said the cornerstone of blunder is plunder back in the
saddle routine regurgitate the color of speed thrum thuck

thwrack Django did the fire enflame your fingers with
divine emanants Pythic embers emblazoned to burn
through stasis dead matter ruminants pedal nugget
endurables quenchers seldom seens seamless seems seeps
inebriate perambulates confiscate cirrhotic redundancies
loams the first heard pedals reminiscence picnics musings by
the shore nuages every cloud a fretboard how much of
music is fingers where in the fingers is the music fingers
with a mind of their own spells musical aptitude envision a
Bill Evans / Django duet yes darling wish you were here love
you too much is made of the comment that the eyes are the
window to the soul be that is it may may we say in our own
way that fingers are the souls fidgets feathers to flutter to fly
the soul about transport which piano player has the
flightiest fingers what do the keys of the piano have in
common with fingers is the hand the window of the finger
the soul of adagio adjacent to wind articulate bring to fret
octave speaking is the tongue the finger of speech the saliva
of soul do glands panic during discord change rhythm
mangle meter so that one bar supports multiple time
signatures entailing a consideration of space which is based

on fit occupation longitude inhabit weather medicine is an exercise in reoccupying space organizing presence prescience performance pugnacity insists constructs derive from construction putting together making assemble the hand is instrumental in making the hand is the soul of making the window to the construct wish you were here another martini sir about the floorboards it would be cheaper to replace them varnish half life fade fidelity festoon recalcitrance stepping on toes flea markets sunsets with broken strings smashed guitars where in the tune is displacement wish you were here on the flip side above perusal below rumination vacation going to from here there where when then this that now back from looking forward killed the weekend travels flaw is you always take you with you where in the voyage is beyond the subject was enterprise overboard above twin 300 hsp evinrude engines sufficient power insures sufficiency big splash speed & the rise of the getaway halfway houses do it by half so much depends upon steatopygia around the bend with little to go on & being out of sorts time assortments aside the incident expired laying blame kept the crumble away who would have thought in the best of times so clearly clean hands soap dirty hands & labor can there be true labor with clean hands perpetuity favors art does true art insist on clean hands bacteria binds with pigment art as insight virus a pledge to the urinal truths establish bellwether the flight was delayed due to the weather geometry a fools rush the tyranny of cards how much of literature is the dependent is the an indicator a pointed finger write a novel titled the your publisher promotes the as the novel of the year the wins the Pulitzer the sales were better than expected the author bathes in the spotlight perplexity is the only subject worth studying with a minor in bewilder who can deny after hour parties allure negligees champagne flutes Bix Beiderbecke ploan high country low soothe voices tarantella feet rapidity beats insipidity during her reign brief but prevalent the color was crimson shot through with rough bark she tantalized life in stages levels first second third floor & such steps back then investigations were more conjure than fact fiction creates magic attracts believers religions are obligated to create believers fiction has worked use it fiction can also create fact can set fact in motion as a matter of fact most facts are fiction true believers aside the function of facts is to securitize fiction here we go loop de loop here we go loop de li the world is everything that is the case Wittgenstein although one could make the case that since it is impossible to identify what is & what is not the case that the world is both what is & what is not the case case worthy is overrated best to say the world is which would of course undermine the viability of philosophy as a profession all those carefully wrought wrung dry divisions highly classified tuck it in cover the sin classification segregates creates mental ghettoes isolates flattens walk your dog bark your car abjure the chore eat meat raw avoid a scuttle prepare your rebuttal five on floor down the corridor the instinct to find origins is but another colonizing reflex the futile search for form form is the uninformed revolt against formlessness civilization is organization dependent specializations tasks haves havenot someofs shipping bill of lading monetary reform health care supply demand taxes schism schema lettering locution weight loss as cultural reflex tea for two tupperware wish you were here otherwise if only than some upon inspection how much of the world is glass removable tumbleweed

toast eggshells circling the national regard its all in the
numbers nimble calculation preoccupation with terminality
goes a long way early dawns the flood that broke the dikes
of the Huang He it was an awful sorrow punishment biceps
& turquoise have a bend to them do clocks sound a death
rattle before they expire a world without sound what would
that look like there is only so much regard one can shed as a
way of forgetting most of modern life designed to abet
forget the forgetful have less to fear on every corner a
pharmacy come back come back Bill Bailey entering the city
of names there is little to prepare for preparation as an art
form formerly served to season approaches to a deepening
condition a legacy of loam a prophesy of stone the
perforation of shadow the impertinence of regularity across
the shores under the borders in the company of throne a
windswept a blather soft pedaling in the company of regal
with too short trousers lest there be moonshine at the party
keep noise to a minimum silence stitched to a storm close
the shutters candle flutter champagne flute beeswax whales
rue the day returning to our theme objectifying noise & its
neuronal reactions cant live in a vacuum but the occupants

beside the case the last car is the quiet car we have choices if only why not could be conditioning points a way habits long embedded change your underwear daily doses to establish method twice a day for the slow of speed not a moment to waste watershed moments if only those & only those on & on it goes logging in with the supposed gospel godspeed get a clue would it were otherwise brotherly with the otherly chums the word name the game blame the same for getting us here the rewind botched advanced conditions hazardous without warning what were your expectations fine station-ery would it were otherwise the advantage of surmise hyper conjecturals keep you sane behind bars scrub behind the ears with each whiff a wham slam the man jam Thelonious I Love You couldnt be otherwise upon the slab after the perforation before the countdown tears cotton down flannel anesthesia Anastasia analgesic proprioception the early stages of Lou Gehrig's disease courtly dances heavy on the violins the hand is mightier than the finger the lung than the tongue upon whose advice with so little to go on the plot thins striates rescinds identifying marks point to an untraceable maker when manufacturing gets in the way

there is always early decision the house ways & means
committee if only & then about some sum of the parts right
of way no turn on red the condition reappears with a
ferocity this time to put at ease mildly we used the lights
changing a bulb no big deal soft preferred does language
bring us closer to the item addressed or push it further apart
of course linguists Chomsky Saussure Sapir Jacobson but
what do they know & do they come at it the right way right
there we have a muddle for what is right about right & that
is what the above are good at scrutinizing is there such a
viable thing as the right the good the just just a matter of
administration & currency exchange in the long run but
does naming a bird breed familiarity intimacy or is it just
that it feels closer more complete more hands on if we can
identify by stamping a name upon is identification the same
as to know does it intrude upon knowing substituting saying
for sentience is saying a form of sentience who says so the
word planted upon the thing arrests the thing in the corral
of stasis or springs the identified more vitally close does the
verb to name have an inevitably contradictory behavior for
it can bring close or it can push away can cocoon a vitality

into a linguistic ghetto or spring to liveliness at a gathering when we encounter a person we do not know but would like to the impulse is to ask for their name as well as offering ones own is the name a corridor to intimacy an opening is offering a name equivalent to a verbal handshake throwing names to the wind the breeze watch the name & the breeze intermingle & wash carry the wind cries Mary you were there all along didnt go anywhere what of it going is overrated staying where you are doesnt get sufficient capital over & over again names pour onto the tongue create a furnace to forge dangerous elaborations if the whole planet refused speech for 24 hours how would that go would that be possible would the written word the text the email be construed as speech a form of there must be some way out of here Burroughs said the way in is the way out wish you were here clandestine in common parlance is a malfunction place your bets even in this moment of pure devotion shavings apprise of a blood solution trading uncertainty for noise extreme Marshall amps acoustic archtops a relic a relish a wish upon a prairie companion anthropological studies strengthen the spine pure solutions seldom have a heartbeat oh Calcutta hesitation before headwinds trades upon senseless rumbling leaves the color of your underwear really matters wish you were here ordinary blends fail to procure good dentition is the dish towel of provision in those moments of pure panic before the flood does anyone care truly care isnt caring a most precious of attributes unadulterated caring packaged in tenderness what is it about tender that wins with care to care be careful caring for they were well cared for cannon the rendition which aborts tradition call upon wise men oranges pineapple pine cedar forests do just find plentiful rain plentiful a loaded word land of plenty plenitude penury impecunious precarious practically speaking stick with plenty plenty of opportunities when opportunity strikes make a run for it the most of you always what can the matter be stay tuned apprise newspapers are filthy being fascinated by connote does not denote ill fitting how are you fixed for change wish it were otherwise the plight the blight too much latitude but if so then otherwise obviously if ever when with little to go on behold betwixt bedizen the border collie bestows friend wore a red scarf unlike any other stroll the sound of

mushroom sizzle preempting the sincerities of squat the
table turned just like that getting along with one another
hardly feasible under the current then it rained the
weatherman smug justified it takes a quill to gander so
much squandered just to qualify the other side of
multiplicity is abound abundance cherish if poetry among
other commotions is a search for truth other than differing
methodologies is it not as much a science as science
equations are tidy mechanisms designed to tidy up
untidynesses a worthy goal for subliminally merited praise
gender pertains to lampposts as urine magnets a top floor
with a view the well cared for connote renditions which
abort tradition hold on hang ten darn dandelion never
abandon futility lacks fever embers away whiplash cardiac
cordial the chips are in recall breathless gills quilt the sky
pentecostal are you hypersensitive or simply fragile
hardiness cannot be overrated all the pills you take cant
prevent the wake wish you were here the livin is easy queasy
spot on breezy a good set of lungs doesnt come cheap
charity aside nowadays the food we eat arrives travel sick
stick close to the soil grow a hoof

Writing Exercise #1:

Roll: Study the snare drum roll. Go back to the earliest practitioners then advance to current time. Choose five drummers, preferably in a time-line, e.g., Baby Dodds, Zutty Singleton, Gene Krupa, Buddy Rich, Max Roach, & study them (in)(ex)tensively. In any musical situation, be able to determine who is performing the roll you are listening to. Once you have absorbed each drummer's distinctive roll sound, write their roll. Write the roll so exhaustively that the reader will be able to hear the roll you are writing.

Your composition will be successful if, after the reader absorbs your written-roll, he / she, upon hearing one of the drummer's roll, can correctly identify which drummer is 'rolling.'

Writing Exercise #2:

Write "Quiet:" Writing 'quiet' does not refer to writing without making a sound, it aspires to illuminate the sound of quiet, its atmosphere, its *feel.*

Quiet is not silence. Silence is the absence of sound. Quiet may bloom in the midst of sound.

Visualize spending a solitary weekend in a mountain cabin. You are in a rocking chair before a roaring fire, you hear the patter of rain on the roof, the windowpane, perhaps you brought your dog who snoozes at your feet, his luxurious exhales lofting like a Persian rug. The sounds in the room might be said to reinforce the quiet.

Back in the city when someone inquires about your weekend, the response: "It was very quiet," is entirely understandable.

Write "quiet."

love seeps

pours pores

dem – on – strates

[percolate peculiar

peristalsis

prompt

blast barrelhouse provocation

bent upon _____ rhapsodic _______

spend expend extend

glee gee glorious glory sheet music

serpentine - - -

spur hieroglyphics parades galore trumpet voluntary

truncheon blade froth rumple rascal pillows aside mount

count – *b r e a t h e* – bunker brood vacate boots a-jive

contrive survive

shoo-fly-shoo

circumstances warrant

the anatomy of breeze

substantiality

voices

in the bone of a pitiful mesh orthodoxy, funereal costs aside,

we prepare for matrimony,

each owns a corridor,

each owns a piece, each-li-ness, cost-effective,

ownership courts the prosperity of flags,

along the fault line

stay in time

in tune

come

be mine

Dearest Lady M', #2

i trust it is not a turn-off that i am a hunting man. & yes, a large buck it was. 1/3 of the meat in the freezer, the other 2 thirds distributed to my closest neighbors. let me assure you, i only kill to eat. & i won't eat meat from an animal that i have not looked in the eye. i use the most primitive weapon: a bare ash longbow with a sapling arrow, — self-made. i am not trying to impress you with my survival skills, just sharing a bit about who i am. also, very much a yes, fresh deer meat is supposed to do wonders for virility. again, not bragging, just wanting to pass along information. do you enjoy cooking? what are a few of your favorite dishes? i know you are very busy because i have not yet received a reply. but i won't let that stop me. reciprocity is overrated. receiving loses its freshness when it comes as a reflex. authenticity is far more precious. when an offering arises from delight rather than obligation. [Max wonders how far he should go with his plans. (He has in mind to build a love-shed on his property (10 acres of mostly woodland), a cozy nest with a large fireplace, voluptuous bedding, & if all goes well, a bear rug he hopes to derive from hunting season in New Jersey). How much should he disclose. He is afraid of pushing her away with too much enthusiasm. Afraid she might feel trapped. Overwhelmed. It is one of those delicate areas in the courtship stage. How to maintain *allure* while erupting with the urge to *devour*].

May I inquire as to your jacket size? Not to moderate the surprise, but I wish to construct a deer-skin jacket for you. [Again, Max is concerned, that he might be overdoing it, over-playing his hand. He can't hold back. Nothing ventured nothing gained. He's never subscribed to restraint.] Also, how do you feel about fringes? It's important to know your preferences, how you think, your *you* off the page, uncorrupted by composition.

Please advise ASAP what dates are best for us to en-gage. I'll be needing to advise Bruce so that his plane will be freed up,

Yours Lovingly,

Max

seep in intervallic residency

c r a w l

space

creat (u)(iv) (r)(i) (e)(ty)

plumb porosity prowl pedal

along the shadow the linger

drifts,

abrasion consorts, . . . granulizes,

. . . spills

the crunch of fire, furs renegade

renown

bristle-lark

smoke-wend slur-flue

soak coalesce

adjutants declare open fire

it's a fine morning

Dear Lady M', #3, nearly 2 months have elapsed since last letter.

[Max is deeply disturbed that he has not heard from M', but knows better than to show it. He has checked with her publisher to validate her email. Whereas under normal circumstances he would laud her not being on Facebook, now it pains as additional distancing].

hope this letter finds you in good spirits. ['Good spirits' is thrown out as bait. he can't imagine she could be thriving without him. He fears she is in trouble]. i enjoyed your recent poems on 'periodicity,' .. . loved that line 'voices of asphodel & alveolus.'

my heart has bloomed since you've been in my life but my writing is suffering. i seem to be all a-jumble, displaced, fidgety. my first novel, *Bella's Dilemma,* was a smash, — you've read it? heard of it, yes? – produced quite a good income followed by a substantial movie deal. my next two novels were flops. i need a winner. the stir you've incited in me, i know it, i just know it, will get the juices going again, . . . will enable us to soar, to lounge on opalescent beaches, to travel, to marinate in each other's skin. [Against his best intentions, Max can no longer hold back, he is too overwrought, too smitten]. why don't we plan to spend a week in Paris letting Lust be our guide, . . . I'll get us a penthouse room with a view of la tour Eiffel, with warm, bubbly-scented water, we'll sip Canard-Duchêne, our eyes will lock, luxuriating in voluptuous splendor while the soles of my feet massage your breasts, tingle across your nipples, teasing them erect, we'll touch, talk, sip, touch, dip closer, ... …

…………………………………

sorry, I'm getting emotional,
write soon,
Max

seep guerrillas in

cunning infiltration

decompose   decentrify   disfigure

de—

ify, →

skid-a-doodle glide

        : the planet has ears :

                tread light:

    : the turn, although not false,

        . . . ineffectual : every alone

                differs:

obscurity revels   axiomatic camouflage

in the chafe of longitude, of stunted

philanthropy, → paired

installments, amphibious matter, permutatory

bedizenings, . . . obligations

tossed,   orthodoxy defiled,

cropped from a failing telemetry

a

saltatory

incipience

seep askew

dis-assembling a-scatter

de-magnetized

un-slung

drawn

to

tatter-rag unknot imperiled

plenish, voided hypertrophies,

prismatic parcel-flutter facet fang,

the

overlooked, the

posturally crimped, the

fallow-sucked;

from the depths of guerilla cunning,

smelt diadem, paw precocity

tantric groundspeak, swells

of

peppering diaspora tremble a

fresh annunciation, a

shared

immaculacy

in the pursuit of

interval

the interstice that wearies

of abandon, of inspecting its

pulse to indispose

the glare ~ ~ ~

such the proposals that

circumflex from twine, that

twist to bombinant alerts in

darkened alveoli, . . .

shuttered

arrhythmic

from seepage this incipience

in the palpitant burl of blastematic

recusance → rogue alerts

→

roustabout groundbreak jigger-swill

so manners

so idylls postscripts trysts moribundity the never-

born the vociferous the accumulating the rectilinear

& the adjacent

with

starfish anemone delinquency

with

co-ag-u- LA-tion pene-TRA-tion perpet-u-A-tion

consultation constitution cuneiform

under the surmise of suppressed regulation egalitarianism

be

damned urban planning be

damned correct pronunciation prevents truancy mural the

frolic anguish   assassins in full

dress maul the mops of decency

everywhere just

so

symbolism

asperity

seep in inveterate dislodge

tilt temptation

aspiration's toil

— turmoil twist

— tarantella tuck

ribbed to an archaic disquiet, sheathed

permeable, squeezed by circumference, by

trellised replica, — inert mold fodder,

fetid fester,

endangered, . . . yet

engendering: perquisite

percolates, groomed

appetitives, feral

fiesta,   fecundity,   draft,

the traffic of

gust

the road to seep road

concourse   coalition

                                        currency

                    conduit

concurrence: gear mesh, crank scuttle,

      rubber / asphalt / bitumen / foot intertangle intercourse

dollop frolic flair

bumps in the road

from _____ to ______

destination: — direction

         — going-ness

   — goal-gridded

        how much of

        'the way to'

is

loss

PRIVATE	BE	ROAD
ROAD	PREPARED	WORK
NO THRU	TO	AHEAD
TRAFFIC	STOP	

privileging traction, . . . access = destiny's

lamentation → alternate route detour,

curves ahead →

where in the

'bend'

is

gradation

puncture to release, to

de-rubber, de-motorize

to

emanate disseminate gestate

gnarled in the bones of signage

squalls from primordial gristle

from → paw fang gullet,

. . . *fur*

from the bellows of a recurring remission this

legion of spheres cylindricals the peat of new geometries of

ratified transpositional glissades leeched to

an

irretrievable

buoyancy

seep in a manner of motion

myrrh myrmidon murmur

m a r c h

mush

un-mire

of wind

aggregate coagulate spurred ungulate

cowled prong

step shuffle slide slip

spli-n-

ter precipitate percipient perforates

pattern abate, uncover color

velocity cilicious stone

plunge succumb

seed

seep in equitable repose

secure of wiggle room

opts for recline, for with-

drawl, a dis-inclination, an

un-

disturb

seep sojourns

loams luxurious luxes in in-

ebriate meander

            sidebar

            succulence

            speculate

spice free when detours fail to accumulate

rocky surfaces become home

boulder free do you contemplate

mercuriality? bulk? condensation?

along the way over the edge repeatedly

voices lose their rasp

turn syrup   hover

luxury brooks no impertinence

disavows compliance

the fairways were bloat utterly

without dodge

ways

never

imagined

seep in eminent domain

authority sweeps fluidic   campaigns

without legs   stamps a

junction for protocol   the chord,

coated with position, fails the

implicit

collared

with comprehension domain

trembles,   develops a fear

of heights,   the unpluggable

now top priority

combustion

reprises

seep in imminent regard

regard: the look strapped with the interrogative,

query calendars

presses

the ruminant

to conceive, . . . conception

  gears solution, quicks

 direction, grids

   appearance,

                                    appearance appears as the locatable,

as manifest, as churn, - - - the assertable

confronts

solubility

seep in plausible deference

along the way:

deft defer re

solve

re

spect

r e n d e r

intone that motion is the prayer, prayer the motion

that the above behind all around remains to

be seen

that your passionate kisses

find no lips

that the blind is your guide

your

syncline

seep champions forage

flutes through furls of

advanced apprehension, through

the weir-wend-wattle wallop of

collapsed itineraries, infested charts,

frayed hobble, to

draw

upon, to fruit, . . . signatories

fuse   to ferret

dis po si tion

that

aroma disposed

to

congrue

January 3, 2020

seep vertigoes

delerials   slipslide   rattle

~~abort~~ shear

axial dislocation

pamutative tilt   shun

cataract anoxia

anoxia →

cyanosis

ataxia

cachexia

leer

skirred

shear

axial shear

skirred

whirligig

clotted with axial

see 1/5

escort

pullulate

whirligig

a ditch of

tossed into the ditch

aporia self-reflective?

Modern physicists framed their accounts of the fundamental nature of things in ~~the~~ language of mathematics.

Is not ~~things~~ attempting to account for the fundamental nature of things through language? Account for as in characterization of the linguistically undocumented? pathos? melancholia?

Dirac trying to find a relativistic quantum theory of the electron

circumnutational gyrate

seep vertigoes

delerials slipslide rattle

ventricular

axial abort

happenstance

pitch whirligig clot cataract ataxia

soundless settles in a throat for comfort

tremble rankles librarians bitten with catalogue

the moment is

fetish

a penny for your thoughts

seep on the lookout

the espy   for

unblemished aperture   for

perfumed pore

                                        pour sanguine

                                        pollen pour

                                        pour sentient

                                        succulence pour

from the outpour of this resuscitance

this gild glitter roar

children badged for rambunction for

erring

the stuff of cloud   of wing

of untethered heedless

from the peppered winds of a romanced latency

a new-bred sobriety

an

unabashed painstaking

seep in immaculate conversion

tetramerous embark & parts yet

to announce themselves, a

sleave of hunches seeking to stitch

the indisputable

quiver

bulk of an indecipherable knowing—

that brazen surety

afloat

seep in jeopardous descent

plunge perilous   steeped in

diffuse   the ooze

                                        that

                                                eludes

antipodal to: the inert, the rawed, the deboned,

the plucked musculatures

poised to: dislodge, delve, dispatch, . . .

hurl   ~   ~

dismembered from tribe, in

the lambent lope of cogitation,

a

dribble

grails

The "Spray" pages are intended to irrigate the text much as a fine mist recirculates to sea. This aspires to a more dynamic interplay than static endnotes.

Spray

Seep Considered

Impinged upon by multiple asphyxiations (i.e., digital tyrannies, ecospheric degradation, technological disruption, threats of nuclear Armageddon), "Seep," here envisioned, is one of the few remaining hygienic pulsations available for evading the ghettoizing binary gridded statistical sterilities intent upon mangling human vitality into frenetic consumption machines.

Seep, in marinated-soak, dribbles   crawls   squirrels *through,* an unhobbled tumbleweed relieved of formulation, impervious to constriction, Seep is the predator of verities, the osmotic ooze,

the creep that credulizes.

Through Considered

Through, as a prime seep-component, ruts for rumination.

through: transition, passage, → flux, development, transformation, a process by which, instrumental, on the way to, vessels, voyages, the road to ____ road.

'To pass through' extends both to access & the pedagogical.

'access' implies a going-through to a where, to a destination, an alternative condition, requirements are accomplished, i.e., 'he went through basic training,' 'when they were through with their loan obligation,' 'we got through the Winter.'

Once 'through,' what then? is through segmental, conditional, intervallic? must a result result? Pedagogical = in the sense of the revelation ensuing from the undertaken. does a through entail a what next? is there a conveyor quality to through? if so, how so? is through destined to be non-autonomous, a contingency? must it remain as interim, souping in evanescence?

Additionally, there is the 'through' of the through-stone which serves to *bind* or strengthen.

In a larger extrapolation, is *through-ness* a central feature of the universe? A variety of Fecundating Rotational Clusters *bounded* by impulse?

Seep Here Installed represents one of Hinge's more extensive efforts to document a Linguistically Undocumented Term. "Linguistically Undocumented" refers to a word's under-recognized, marginal, borderline status. Similarly to a Film Documentary, these applications seek to deliver the specific facticities of its subject matter. The Documental Tool of Hinge is Language. It can often feel like we are witnessing 'seep' unravel in slow motion as its very DNA rifles across the page. Or as Jonathan Mulcahy-King puts it in the February 2018 issue of *X-Peri*:

"The uniqueness of Hinging—as a post-language innovation can be found in its unwavering study of the term (a given word) through its 'application.' In doing so, the hingist approaches a term as an archaeologist might a fossil or artefact—it is dug up, analysed, chipped away at, an inventory is made, it is carbon-dated and processed for vital information, a representation is made to project its innate potential etc. In this sense, Hinge does for the word what BpNichol did for the letter (See "H: An Excursion" bpNichol Archive), it poeticizes and re-presents language as a chain of information, moving reflexively as it navigates through the 'beautiful quixotic.' This is unique as Hinge is attempting a full-scale poetic study of the term, and as a starting point, this is certainly intriguing, producing poems / applications based around the terms 'askew,' 'seepage,' 'pathos,' 'glide,' 'meander,' for example, means language is actually Hinging with itself, and the Hingist, is merely an observer, a scientist."

31 **Tercaquarium** refers to tercets parading in a textual aquarium.

38 **Birds are flowers ... birds** is a two-line koan by A.R. Ammons which attracted me until I recited it to Dr. Mary Newell who said "that comparison seems to promote a static visual image as the full signification. It's like looking at a bird through a window, at a *distance.* Flowers open up to complete their life cycle. Consider Dickinson's 'Split the lark and you'll find the music': a bird opened would lose its

song, whereas an opening flower offers its scent." The following day I presented her with my version: "birds are birds / & flowers are flowers."

53 **folly for to seem** teems from "Comment dire / what is the word," Samuel Beckett's final written work. It is clear that the importance of music on Beckett's work was profound: he had more close friends among musicians than writers. At home he would play Chopin waltzes & sonatas, Schubert's "Impromptus," Haydn sonatas, Beethoven & others. I found it curious that in neither of the two main Beckett biographies does it ever mention any involvement Nor any interest in Jazz which is conspicuous because in the 40's & 50's Paris had become the new world capital of Jazz. Sartre, Beauvoir, Merleau-Ponty, Camus, among others, were feasting on Miles, Gillespie, Louis Armstrong, Django et. al. For someone who felt that "music was the art form that came the closest to pure spirit," what does it indicate that this vital fount of psychic farming was avoided? Since Beckett often used musical terms like "fortissimo," "cadenza," "da capo" in directing his plays, what would his plays be like if he had been working off of a more jazz-based consciousness? After reading "what is the word," It occurred to me to write the same text (meaning reproducing only those words in the Beckett poem) from a more jazz-based consciousness. Also noteworthy in the spirit of creative recirculation is that "afaint afar away" are the final words of Joyce's *Finnegans Wake.*

56 **passage: let us pause:** is pause an essential element in developmental passage? The reader is encouraged to spend some time exploring the dictionary definition of 'pass.'

The rumination over the word 'passage' also initializes the meta-poem (see below '61 rumination upon') by, in this case, plucking out a vital component of the composition & exposing it to further examination.

56 **to de-fixate the term:** 'term' is the Hinge term used for the word that is undergoing investigation. It would be interchangeable with 'subject.'

56 **when he 'passes' the baton to another runner:** to behave analogously to the 'term,' the baton would mutate, shape-shift, re-color, & re-compose with each hand-off.

67 **impulse is to release, — to splinter/spill/slip:** See *LinguaQuake* (Black Widow Press) p.191, spray note #6.

74 **brood in attenuate fever diagnosed** was spurred while sharing the poem with Mary Newell & realizing the improbability of anyone understanding how truly concrete the poem was, how every word could be accounted for. She advised me to write about it. To illustrate my intention to muscularize the non-configured.

76 **brood quicks from the folds of despair** is in the form of a Petrarchan sonnet.

80 **rumination upon:** the idea of poetic *rumination* is being proposed as a meta-poem, as the ability to densify the application with another layer (or layers) of investigation. It should aspire not to commentary, but to further magnify the volumetric presence & fleshing-out of the subject matter.

194 **Results** resulted from a chapbook invitation from Trainwreck Press. My first thought was to publish a "seep" sequence but was worried that it might conflict with my upcoming "seep" volume from Black Widow Press. Wondering what to submit, whether or not "seep" should be vetoed, "results" slammed into my psyche.

I envisioned a 25 page verbal spontaneous rush which would be free of the currently popular trend of typographical "décor" so facilely enabled on today's computers. This was a project with constraints:

I would insist that the unadorned 'word' carry the day void of any ornamental flourishes; minimal punctuation would be permitted.

In this age of distraction & ready convenience, I felt this approach would force a deeper responsibility on the language, that by reducing the text to the purely lingual, the pressure for the word to perform at full capacity would be unconditional.

'Results' is in continuance.

221 **skid-a-doodle glide:** for a fuller inspection of 'glide,' see *Un*—(Black Widow Press) pp. 162–164.

The following 'seeps' have yet to announce themselves &

invite participation.

. seep reconsiders

. seep remonstrates

. seep demonstrates

. seep relocates

. seep resists

. seep relishes

. seep circumambulates

. seep construes

. seep constrains

. seep abstains

. seep muses

. seep bemuses

. seep misconstrues

. seep fantasizes

. seep extrapolates

. seep determines

. seep foresees

. seep improvises

. seep polishes

. seep redeems

. seep peremptorizes

. seep extemporizes

. seep hibernates

. seep migrates

. seep approaches the human nerve domain

. seep concerns itself with fructose

. seep aligns itself with alien attributes

. seep resides in the theater of doubt

. seep consumes the lion's share of ambidexterity

. seep defies digital tyranny

(To suggest just a few)

The originator of Hinge Theory, HELLER LEVINSON lives in New York.

TITLES FROM BLACK WIDOW PRESS

TRANSLATION SERIES

Approximate Man and Other Writings by Tristan Tzara. Translated and edited by Mary Ann Caws.

Art Poétique by Guillevic. Translated by Maureen Smith.

The Big Game by Benjamin Péret. Translated with an introduction by Marilyn Kallet.

Boris Vian Invents Boris Vian: A Boris Vian Reader. Edited and translated by Julia Older.

Capital of Pain by Paul Eluard. Translated by Mary Ann Caws, Patricia Terry, and Nancy Kline.

Chanson Dada: Selected Poems by Tristan Tzara. Translated with an introduction and essay by Lee Harwood.

Earthlight (Clair de Terre) by André Breton. Translated by Bill Zavatsky and Zack Rogow. (New and revised edition.)

Essential Poems and Prose of Jules Laforgue. Translated and edited by Patricia Terry.

Essential Poems and Writings of Joyce Mansour: A Bilingual Anthology. Translated with an introduction by Serge Gavronsky.

Essential Poems and Writings of Robert Desnos: A Bilingual Anthology. Edited with an introduction and essay by Mary Ann Caws.

EyeSeas (Les Ziaux) by Raymond Queneau. Translated with an introduction by Daniela Hurezanu and Stephen Kessler.

Fables in a Modern Key by Pierre Coran. Translated by Norman R. Shapiro. Full-color illustrations by Olga Pastuchiv.

Fables of Town & Country by Pierre Coran. Translated by Norman R. Shapiro. Full-color illustrations by Olga Pastuchiv.

A Flea the Size of Paris: The Old French Fatrasies & Fatras. Edited and translated by Ted Byrne and Donato Mancini.

Forbidden Pleasures: New Selected Poems 1924–1949 by Luis Cernuda. Translated by Stephen Kessler.

Furor and Mystery & Other Writings by René Char. Translated by Mary Ann Caws and Nancy Kline.

The Gentle Genius of Cécile Périn: Selected Poems (1906–1956). Edited and translated by Norman R. Shapiro.

Guarding the Air: Selected Poems of Gunnar Harding. Translated and edited by Roger Greenwald.

Howls & Growls: French Poems to Bark By. Translated by Norman R. Shapiro; illustrated by Olga K. Pastuchiv.

I Have Invented Nothing: Selected Poems by Jean-Pierre Rosnay. Translated by J. Kates.

In Praise of Sleep: Selected Poems of Lucian Blaga Translated with an introduction by Andrei Codrescu.

The Inventor of Love & Other Writings by Gherasim Luca. Translated by Julian & Laura Semilian. Introduction by Andrei Codrescu. Essay by Petre Răileanu.

Jules Supervielle: Selected Prose and Poetry. Translated by Nancy Kline & Patricia Terry.

La Fontaine's Bawdy by Jean de La Fontaine. Translated with an introduction by Norman R. Shapiro.

Last Love Poems of Paul Eluard. Translated with an introduction by Marilyn Kallet.

A Life of Poems, Poems of a Life by Anna de Noailles. Edited and translated by Norman R. Shapiro. Introduction by Catherine Perry.

Love, Poetry (L'amour la poésie) by Paul Eluard. Translated with an essay by Stuart Kendall.

Pierre Reverdy: Poems, Early to Late. Translated by Mary Ann Caws and Patricia Terry.

Poems of André Breton: A Bilingual Anthology. Translated with essays by Jean-Pierre Cauvin and Mary Ann Caws.

Poems of A.O. Barnabooth by Valery Larbaud. Translated by Ron Padgett and Bill Zavatsky.

Poems of Consummation by Vicente Aleixandre. Translated by Stephen Kessler.

Préversities: A Jacques Prévert Sampler. Translated and edited by Norman R. Shapiro.

RhymAmusings (AmuseRimes) by Pierre Coran. Translated by Norman R. Shapiro.

The Sea and Other Poems by Guillevic. Translated by Patricia Terry. Introduction by Monique Chefdor.

Through Naked Branches by Tarjei Vesaas. Translated, edited, and introduced by Roger Greenwald.

To Speak, to Tell You? Poems by Sabine Sicaud. Translated by Norman R. Shapiro. Introduction and notes by Odile Ayral-Clause.

MODERN POETRY SERIES

BARNSTONE, WILLIS.
ABC of Translation
African Bestiary (forthcoming)

BRINKS, DAVE.
The Caveat Onus
The Secret Brain: Selected Poems 1995–2012

CESEREANU, RUXANDRA.
Crusader-Woman. Translated by Adam J. Sorkin. Introduction by Andrei Codrescu.
Forgiven Submarine by Ruxandra Cesereanu and Andrei Codrescu.

ESHLEMAN, CLAYTON.
An Alchemist with One Eye on Fire
Anticline
Archaic Design
Clayton Eshleman/The Essential Poetry: 1960–2015
Grindstone of Rapport: A Clayton Eshleman Reader
Penetralia
Pollen Aria
The Price of Experience
Endure: Poems by Bei Dao. Translated by Clayton Eshleman and Lucas Klein.
Curdled Skulls: Poems of Bernard Bador. Translated by Bernard Bador with Clayton Eshleman.

JORIS, PIERRE.
Barzakh (Poems 2000–2012)
Exile Is My Trade: A Habib Tengour Reader

KALLET, MARILYN.
How Our Bodies Learned
The Love That Moves Me
Packing Light: New and Selected Poems
Disenchanted City (La ville désenchantée) by Chantal Bizzini. Translated by J. Bradford Anderson, Darren Jackson, and Marilyn Kallet.

KELLY, ROBERT.
Fire Exit
The Hexagon

KESSLER, STEPHEN.
Garage Elegies

LAVENDER, BILL.
Memory Wing

LEVINSON, HELLER.
from stone this running
LinguaQuake
Seep
Tenebraed
Un-
Wrack Lariat

OLSON, JOHN.
Backscatter: New and Selected Poems
Dada Budapest
Larynx Galaxy

OSUNDARE, NIYI.
City Without People: The Katrina Poems

ROBERTSON, MEBANE.
An American Unconscious
Signal from Draco: New and Selected Poems

ROTHENBERG, JEROME.
Concealments and Caprichos
Eye of Witness: A Jerome Rothenberg Reader. Edited with commentaries by Heriberto Yepez & Jerome Rothenberg.
The President of Desolation & Other Poems

SAÏD, AMINA.
The Present Tense of the World: Poems 2000–2009. Translated with an introduction by Marilyn Hacker.

SHIVANI, ANIS.
Soraya (Sonnets)

WARD, JERRY W., JR.
Fractal Song

ANTHOLOGIES / BIOGRAPHIES

Barbaric Vast & Wild: A Gathering of Outside and Subterranean Poetry (Poems for the Millennium, vol. 5). Editors: Jerome Rothenberg and John Bloomberg-Rissman

Clayton Eshleman: The Whole Art by Stuart Kendall

Revolution of the Mind: The Life of André Breton by Mark Polizzotti